JOSHUA LEEDS

...er of Sound: How to Manage Your Personal Soundscape for a ... Productive, and Healthy Life

...hemy: Conversations with Leading Sound Practitioners

...a Dog's Ear: Music to Calm Your Canine Companion (... 1–2)

...a Dog's Ear: Music for the Canine Household (Vols. 1–2)

...De-Stress (Dr. Andrew Weil's *Music for Self-Healing* series)

...Vitality (Dr. Andrew Weil's *Music for Self-Healing* series)

...ntial Sound Series (8-CD set)

...th

...ning Program (8-CD set)

...ody, Sound Mind: Music for Healing, with Andrew Weil, MD

...ditations for Optimum Health, with Andrew Weil, MD

...nd Health Series (6-CD set)

...Garden for Concentration, with The Monroe Institute

...orks for Relaxation, with The Monroe Institute

...y for Louise

...e Present, with Louise L. Hay

...Affirmation, with Louise L. Hay

through a
Dog's Ear

Using Sound to Improve
the Health & Behavior
of Your Canine Companion

JOSHUA LEEDS
&
SUSAN WAGNER, DVM, MS

SOUNDS TRUE
Boulder, Colorado

Sounds True, Inc., Boulder CO 80306

Published 2008
Printed in Canada
✪ This book is printed on recycled paper containing
100% post-consumer waste and processed without chlorine.

10 9 8 7 6 5 4 3 2 1

Library of Congress Cataloging-in-Publication Data

Leeds, Joshua.
  Through a dog's ear : using sound to improve the health and behavior
of your canine companion / Joshua Leeds & Susan Wagner.
       p. cm.
  Includes bibliographical references and index.
  ISBN 978-1-59179-811-8 (hardcover)
  1. Dogs—Behavior. 2. Dogs—Health. 3. Dogs—Physiology. 4.
Dogs—Effect of sound on. 5. Sound—Physiological effect. I. Wagner,
Susan, 1957- II. Title.

SF433.L44 2008
636.7'0887—dc22

                                    2007046178

Book design by Karen Polaski

Photo on page 3 by Margaret Tucker. Photo on page 8 by Trevor James Ingraham.
Photo on page 11 by Lisa Spector. Photo on page 42 by Joshua Leeds. Photo on page 51
by D. Wade. Photo on page 73 by Heather at Cleland Animal Park. Photo on page 157
by Lyric Tucker-Leeds. Photo on page 158 by Ellen S. Whittle.

Excerpt on pages 25–26 is from How to Be Your Dog's Best Friend (Revised) by The Monks
of New Skete. Copyright © 1978, 2002 by The Monks of New Skete. By permission of
LITTLE, BROWN & COMPANY

> **Note to the reader:** this book is intended as an informational guide.
> The applications, approaches, and techniques described herein are not
> a substitute for professional veterinary or medical care.

The Music of Through a Dog's Ear
The enclosed CD contains selections from two music compilations, Music to Calm Your
Canine Companion, Vols. 1 & 2, and Music for the Canine Household. This music has been
clinically tested and shown to calm dogs. Information on the use of this starter CD
can be found on page 119. Research findings are available on page 77 and online at
ThroughADogsEar.com.

For a free catalog of wisdom teachings for the inner life,
call 800-333-1985 or visit www.SoundsTrue.com

Dedicated to my ever-wiser sister,

Ronna Alyse,

for her love of all living things.

—Joshua Leeds

This book is dedicated

with love and gratitude

to Dr. Pamela Chen.

We miss you.

—Susan Wagner

Contents

Acknowledgments

LISA SPECTOR, a concert pianist residing in Half Moon Bay, California, was the singular impetus for our exploration of the effect of music and sound on our canine companions. Long ago, she made a simple request: "How about a CD to sell at my local pet shop?" Two years of research, eight hours of newly recorded music, an in-depth book, and published research finally manifests that presumably simple CD inquiry. Lisa's love of music is equaled only by her love for dogs. *Through a Dog's Ear* finally connects these objects of her affection, and dog guardians everywhere are better for it. Our heartfelt gratitude goes to you, dear and patient Lisa!

Annie Brody has been a steady and true anchor in our sea of exploration and was the creator of our wonderful title. Her dedication to a higher awareness of human/animal relating is not only inspiring, but graces the pages of this book. Brava!

We gratefully acknowledge the brilliant sound researcher, Dr. Alfred Tomatis (1920–2001), who surely would have loved seeing his great discoveries about therapeutic sound being applied to four-leggeds as well as their people.

To our publisher, Sounds True, we are so privileged to be included among the important contributions you bring to the world. Fond thanks to Tami Simon, Tara Lupo, Kelly Notaras, Chantal Pierrat, Shelly Vickroy, Jennifer Coffee, Karen Polaski, Beverly Yates, Deidre Saddoris, Aron Arnold, Elisabeth Rinaldi, and countless others, including the many beloved Sounds True dogs!

Thanks to Stephen Topping for his magnificent editing and his caring, which was often way beyond the call of duty; to Amanda Jones, photographer, for the heartfelt images; to Dr. Deborah Wells, of Queen's University, Belfast, for providing encouragement and strong scientific shoulders for us to stand upon; to Sandy Rogers for her inspirational insight into the world of dogs; and to our wonderful publicist, Jane Rohman, thank you for the great effort and results.

Dr. Susan Wagner would like to thank Sebastian and Sammy for the joy they gave; Vinny, for holding down the fort, and Buster, for strengthening its boundaries; her family, both biological and of *other* mothers; her father, Don Orbovich, for making all of this possible. Heartfelt thanks to husband, Rich, for his eternal love and support.

Special gratitude to Dr. Tony Buffington for his valued friendship and expertise, and a deeply felt appreciation to Traci Shreyer, MA, Animal Applied Behaviorist, without whom the writing of chapters 8–9 would not have been possible.

Joshua Leeds sends heartfelt gratitude to Rachel Leeds for a lifetime of encouragement, and for demonstrating how an inherited terrier named Sidney could become a best friend. Sisters Sharon, Deborah, and mama's boy wanna-be, Ronna B.—your lifetime of combined support is without measure.

Sanda Jasper, who so gracefully helps me stay on target. Sheila Smith Allen for generosity of spirit and keeping me honest with the details.

Margaret Tucker, who loved and healed Rita the Akita and others of close heart. Lyric Kaela Grace, my beautiful daughter, for learning and teaching the healing power of an animal's love. Acknowledgment and deep appreciation to Kiki La Porta for all her best efforts. Lastly, to my main pup, Obus—cherished and never forgotten.

A New Sound Awareness

When I first visited New York City, my fiancée proudly greeted me with Rita, her cherished year-old Japanese Akita. A statuesque and soulful dog of nearly 100 pounds, Rita was just what Margaret needed: a business watchdog, a protector while walking the Manhattan streets, and a truly faithful, loving companion.

"Be careful when you let her off the leash," was the only warning—a caution that rang in my ears a few weeks later as I permitted Rita to walk unencumbered through Riverside Park. This little bit of green was Rita's favorite haunt, just a few blocks from our apartment. Our experience, like that of most dog walkers, was that our dog loved her few minutes of freedom from human restriction. She would get a little skittish at times, but would always come when called. That night, however, all it took was the sound from an unseen car's tailpipe backfiring to send Rita off like a shot, running frantically for the safety of home. The only problem was four lanes of fast yellow taxis on Broadway between the park and our apartment.

"Rita! Rita! Rita!" I screamed as I ran after her in the chilly night. She was one block ahead and fast outpacing me. Two blocks later, I was still running as fast as I could after Rita, who was running as fast as she could toward Broadway.

"Riiiitttttaaaaaa!"

Suddenly there was the sound of horns, followed by skidding tires, a loud *whack!,* and then that pit-in-the-stomach quiet—the kind of stillness where everything starts going in slow motion. As I turned the corner, my worst nightmare awaited me. Rita was motionless on the asphalt, a taxi driver who didn't speak English was gesturing wildly, and people were coming out of the shops and restaurants to see what had happened.

When I reached her side, I looked for movement in her belly—for any sign of breath. *Yes!* She was still breathing. Next, I looked into her eyes but didn't get the same reassurance—they were wide open, watering, and full of fear, pain, and I don't know what. I shouted out a telephone number and a neighbor called my fiancée, who arrived within moments. She placed gentle and quivering hands on Rita's face, running them slowly down her neck and body. No blood or exposed bones, thank goodness—a miracle, considering the size of the dent Rita had left on the yellow taxi, which had now left us alone in the middle of the street. We put Rita's leash back on and slowly coaxed her back to her feet. She could stand up—sort

Rita the Akita with Lyric Tucker-Leeds

of—and we helped her into another cab. Eight long minutes later, Rita hobbled into the emergency animal hospital for x-rays and observation and, for us, an anxious night of waiting.

Rita came home the next evening with lots of pain medication and a diagnosis of severely bruised ribs but no apparent organ damage. Because of her size and young age, she had miraculously survived being hit at 40 miles per hour! Many years later, we discovered that several of her vertebrae had fused together due to the injury. Nonetheless, Rita lived almost a full decade after the accident.

For years, when I thought back on that most painful Manhattan night, I wondered how it was possible that one seemingly insignificant and distant sound could have shocked such a large, professionally trained animal into bolting for home. What went through this dog's ear? It took me two decades to figure it out. Although powerful and large, Rita was high-strung; she had a very sensitive nervous system. And as with people who are "sensitive" to noise, it didn't take much to upset her balance and cause her to seek the shelter of home.

CANINES IN THE COAL MINE

As Rita's accident illustrates, over-stimulation of auditory senses can have as significant an effect on our animals as it does on humans. While there is no official diagnosis of "noise disease," millions of people suffer from dysfunctional auditory processing or from the inability to control their environments. *Through a Dog's Ear* explores a similarity between human and canine auditory perception, and investigates the effects of the human soundscape on our canine companions.

I am privileged to write this book with Dr. Susan Wagner, veterinary neurologist, academician, and holistic practitioner of animals *and* humans. Her focus on the spiritual nature of animals and the connection between human and animal welfare issues informs her perspective throughout.

In *Through a Dog's Ear,* we explore what's known about sound and dogs, compare current research into music and canine behavior, and begin the process of connecting the dots of a picture that has not been painted before. In the end, the picture reveals a new kind of canary in the coal mine: the behavioral problems in our dogs forewarn of a much larger problem in the human soundscape, a problem that is affecting us as much as it influences them. In fact, we believe that many anxiety behaviors common in both the American people *and* their dogs may be the result of cumulative sensory overload, starting with the sound environments in which we live.

Is it possible that the uptick in psychological and physiological dysfunctions we're now observing in the canine population may be a reaction to our ever more media-driven, high-tech, 24-7 culture? Is this same environment a direct cause of the increased spread of stress- and environment-related maladies in humans, as well?

Research has shown that dogs are among the most adaptable of animals. Most dog guardians have thus assumed that it is the dog's job to adjust to whatever environment we offer them—no matter how stressful. In this case, perhaps our dogs' willingness to do anything for us has become their Achilles' heel—the result of their total compliance is that canines are more stressed than ever before.

CANINE BEHAVIORAL ISSUES: AN OVERWHELMING PROBLEM?

As many as 90 percent of people who bring their dogs to a vet discuss some type of canine behavioral issue.[1] Dog behavior problems range from mild anxiety to severe aggression. Estimates suggest that more than ten million dogs have separation anxiety.[2] To put this in perspective, one out of every seven American dogs currently suffers when left alone or separated from their main person(s).

At the opposite end of the behavioral spectrum is aggression, a complex issue. In 1994, an estimated 4.7 million Americans were bitten, with 6,000 hospitalized.[3]

> The link between interpersonal violence and animal cruelty is an area important to the authors and worthy of everyone's attention. If you would like to learn more, visit www.ThroughADogsEar.com.

Through a Dog's Ear suggests that we examine our environments to determine if we are creating the best sensory space possible to support behavioral balance and health in our dogs—and, subsequently, in ourselves. These concepts should not be construed as a pampering; rather, they are about finding solutions to the growing problem of constant stimulation—an issue few have recognized. Who would have thought that simplified music could be part of the solution for de-stressing our best furry friends?

PSYCHOACOUSTICS MEETS BIOACOUSTICS

An official definition of psychoacoustics is "a branch of science dealing with hearing, the sensations produced by sounds, and the problems of communication."[4] Psychoacoustics may also be thought of as "the study of the perception of sound."

As a psychoacoustician, I study the effect of sound on the human nervous system. After a few decades of research and observation, I know that auditory input has a much larger impact on the psyche and body than most people think. When our auditory process is under- or overwhelmed, or when we have difficulty processing sound properly, there can be multiple and far-reaching ramifications.[5] One of the profound joys I have found in the clinical studies of music for dogs is the discovery that many of the same principles and effects of sound are shared by people *and* animals. This reinforces what soundworkers already know—that sound is a potent energy that is not to be taken for granted.

Over the last fifty years, musicians, producers, and therapeutic professionals have clarified and innovated music and sound techniques that naturally affect our human body pulses—brain waves, heart rate, and breath. We've learned to *play* the human body in a purposeful way. By adding the natural processes of *resonance* (the ability of one vibration to alter another), *entrainment* (the effect of periodic rhythms to speed up or slow down the brain, heart, and breath), and auditory *pattern identification*[6] (determining when it is conducive for the brain to be in an active or passive mode) to the musical palette of harmony, melody, and form, it is now possible to create potent soundtracks for specific purposes.

But what does psychoacoustics have to do with the health and well-being of our canine companions? This is where *bioacoustics* comes into play. The Acoustical Society of America defines *animal bioacoustics* as the study of sound in non-human animals.[7] Like psychoacoustics, it is a branch of science that deals with the relation between living beings and sound.[8] That said, bioacoustics is not a field I ever expected to find myself studying. But when a remarkable woman and her even more remarkable dog showed up on my doorstep, everything changed.

HOW THE MUSIC AND BOOK CAME TO BE

In 2003, concert pianist Lisa Spector and her puppy, Señor Sanchez, attended one of my lectures. Lisa telephoned me soon after. "How about making an album of classical music for dogs?" she asked.

Señor Sanchez and Lisa Spector

An avid dog lover, she had raised puppies for Guide Dogs for the Blind and witnessed a profound effect on the dogs when she played her nine-foot Steinway. Instead of looking for puppy trouble, rambunctious sixteen-week-olds would tumble under the piano in a furry clump and fall into calm and gentle sleep.

While the image was adorable, I was not sure about Lisa's request. After twenty years of hard work, I could see my reputation quickly going, as they say, to the dogs. I figured if I did this, I'd probably be struck by the wrath of Bach or Beethoven. After all, these were serious guys who wrote music for God—not dogs!

As crazy as it was, the idea stuck with me. Intrigued, I went to a local university to see if there was any research on the effect of music on animals. Reading abstracts for two days can be a dry and laborious process, but the data I found (or more often than not, couldn't find), was compelling enough to propel me even further down the path—to a veterinary university a hundred miles away.

After another few days of picking through complex databases, I was hooked. I learned that:

- Country music calmed ponies
- Country music best brought cows home
- Classical music made cows produce more milk
- Dolphins swam in exuberant synchrony to Bach
- Classical music improved the growth rate in chickens

- Classical music caused hens to feed more
- Classical music relaxed dogs

It is interesting to note that in these research results, rock music and jazz were often the styles that got the least desirable results from the animals.

THE MUSICAL PREFERENCES OF DOGS

While interested and amused at how classical and country music were sweeping the animal music awards, I became aware of the lack of credible research into the effect of resonance (tone) and entrainment (rhythm) on domesticated animals. However, once I found the research of Irish animal behaviorist Dr. Deborah Wells,[9] I knew there were truly interesting possibilities in creating music that would positively affect our animal friends.

Wells's 2002 study, conducted in dog shelters in San Francisco and Northern Ireland, found that classical music created notable relaxation in canines, while heavy metal music resulted in more agitated behavior.

Dr. Wells concluded: "It is well established that music can influence our moods. Classical music, for example, can help to reduce levels of stress, whilst grunge music can promote hostility, sadness, tension and fatigue. *It is now believed that dogs may be as discerning as humans when it comes to musical preference* [italics ours]."

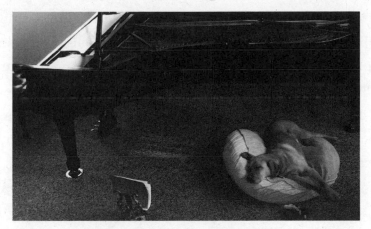

Sanchez listening deeply to Schubert

Dogs and musical preference? This was the missing piece I was looking for. With a notebook of research in hand, I consented to give the music for dogs project a try. I was curious to find out if the psychoacoustic techniques that I'd honed so effectively with people could also be effective with dogs.

I was still a little dubious because I had never noticed any indication that dogs engaged with music—I'd never seen a dog pant, tap a paw, or even wag a tail in rhythm. Would it be possible to change a dog's heart rate or brainwaves with the use of external rhythms, as is easily done with people? I figured I would give it a try.

ALL CLASSICAL MUSIC ISN'T THE SAME

The objective was clear: create psychoacoustically designed soundtracks for calming and reducing anxiety. In most instances, dogs don't need to be stimulated or aroused; rather, they need to be soothed and slowed down. I had long been accomplishing the same for their guardians by designing soundtracks based on a spectrum I call *simple sound.*

I believe that when a nervous system (canine, human, or other) is compromised, overwhelmed, or stressed, its ability to process sensory data is diminished. I also believe, thanks to the discoveries of ground-breaking sound researcher Alfred Tomatis, MD, that sound is a nutrient for the nervous system. The idea, then, is to create soundtracks that are easy for the nervous system to absorb; it's important to provide enough sound, but not to overdo it. I work with the concept of *regulation of sensory data*—being intentional with how much information is being sent to the brain. In the case of a stressed nervous system, slow and simplified sound input is enough to charge the nervous system but not too much to make it tune out. This sonic recipe is simple sound.

To accomplish this task for dogs, Lisa and I began by selecting the style of music we thought most appropriate. The classical genre is easy on the nervous system because the form and patterns are easy to perceive—be it baroque, classical, or romantic. This simplicity allows for passive hearing (vs. active listening) to take place.

Lisa and I first picked selections that were intrinsically simple in orchestration and arrangement. When we got into more complex pieces, we would modify arrangements by changing tempo, removing entire harmonic sections if they were too complex, or using different orchestration to regulate the amount of high and low frequencies. In some instances, we would repeat sections to create a deeper entrainment and patterning effect. While we would sometimes remove sections of music, we never added any notes of our own making. It was not necessary; the classical masters created all the beauty and harmony we needed. Our goal was only to make the music as easily processed by the brain as possible.

We then recorded four albums of varying complexity, tempo, and orchestration. Using the simple sound spectrum, we worked along a continuum moving from fast, high, and complex to slower, lower, and more simple.

Many pieces were performed with solo piano while others included cello, oboe, and English horn. In keeping with the concept of auditory data regulation, a solo instrument usually requires the least amount of neurological processing. Solo piano is a great choice for this objective if the arrangements are not too complex. The choice of cello and oboe was based on sonorities: cello offers lower tones, while oboe provides the high frequencies. Together, this orchestration made for a warm and wonderful confluence of tones. My sole caveat for the project was that the music we were creating would be psychoacoustically relevant to humans in addition to dogs. Not knowing what the canine effect would be, I needed to hedge my bets on what was turning out to be an ever-expanding investment of time and energy.[10]

The results of our efforts are included on the starter CD that accompanies this book. In coming chapters, we'll further discuss the specifics about how the music was designed and created, and how you can best use the musical selections to calm and soothe your canine companion.

During this period, I received an inquiry from a veterinary neurologist in Ohio. Not only was she a vet who studied the brain, but she was also an integrative doctor—combining the best of Western veterinary medicine with complementary energy healing processes. Dr. Susan Wagner was looking for music to be used in a research study on the effect of music on dogs with epilepsy. I was looking for someone who could help me understand the "how, what, and why" of dog hearing. It was a match made in heaven. I mentioned the project Lisa and I were working on, and my then-unbeknown co-author-to-be agreed to create a pilot research project. That was a synchronistic and wonderfully pivotal day.

Within a year, using the music Lisa and I had created, Dr. Wagner prodigiously coordinated the testing of more than 150 dogs in animal shelters, veterinary clinics, service dog organizations, grooming facilities, and private homes. Her findings were unexpected and extraordinary. Whereas the 2002 Wells study had found classical to be the most effective music of three different types—pop, classical, and heavy metal—Dr. Wagner discovered that not all classical music produces the same effects.

Psychoacoustically designed classical music was more effective at inducing canine relaxation and sleep and doubled the abatement of canine anxiety behaviors.

One of the most exciting findings of Dr. Wagner's study was that the same music that calms dogs also helps people relax. Each of the four albums used in the study had decent outcomes. However, the single album that caused eyebrow-raising canine results was an album that had been specifically designed for industrial-strength people calming. More details about the research into music and dogs can be found in chapter 7, "Breakthrough Research."

What does it mean that the same music that had such a deep effect on people also worked with dogs? How does this factor into the human-animal experience? Dr. Wagner and I believe that this territory has much to teach us; many of the answers we seek will be found in the coming chapters.

ॐ

In the broader scope, sound is only one form of sensory integration that may be affecting your dogs, along with sight, smell, taste, touch, and movement. We believe that canines—be they normal, sensitive, or troubled—need to be observed and treated from many different points of view. Therefore, while sound is our primary focal point, you will also find additional sensory suggestions to enhance the well-being of your beloved companions.

A final note before we begin. *Through a Dog's Ear* is not simply a dog book. This is a dog and human book. After extensive research and exploration, Dr. Wagner and I have come to understand that there is no way to have a discussion about dog behavior or health without taking into account the role that humans play in a dog's life. Dogs and people cannot be divorced. Over the course of twelve millennia, our species have grown ever more dependent upon each other—they need us and we *really* need them. Our dogs consistently remind us of the power of unconditional love and companionship and clearly we respond to this. Otherwise, why would there be 75 million dogs in this country?

—Joshua Leeds

San Francisco

August 2007

CHAPTER 1

Petey,
Shut Up!

L isa is a concert pianist who loves dogs. While on tour, she was staying with a local family that had two dogs and an African gray parrot. Willie, the Dalmatian, had his favorite piano pieces, which he clearly recognized. He did not care for Bach or Mozart, it seems, because he always left the room when they were played. One day Lisa was preparing for a concert by practicing Grieg's Piano Concerto, apparently one of Willie's favorites, as he began to bellow with delight. However, as soon as Willie started howling, the family's little dog, Petey, started barking incessantly and the parrot began shrieking, "Petey, shut up! Petey, shut up!" This happened every time Lisa played Grieg.

Jake, a faithful Labrador/Golden Retriever mix, would lie at his master's feet. Ben would sing—and most of the time Jake would moan. But whenever Ben sang "Lover, Come Back to Me,"[1] Jake would spring up and bark along—every time, like clockwork. One Fourth of July, the sound of nearby fireworks frightened Jake so badly that he ran away. It took a nerve-wracking two days to bring him home. Ben whistled "Lover, Come Back to Me" while he and his family combed local neighborhoods until they finally found Jake, shaking and whimpering, on a dark porch two miles away. He recognized the song and gave a half-tired bark. But it was enough.

Then, there's Peter's one-hundred-pound male Doberman Pinscher, Charles, who was as gentle as could be. He would sleep quietly whenever someone played music on the piano. But when the children pounded on the keyboard in a random and chaotic manner, Charles would stroll over and stand between the kids and the instrument patiently waiting until someone agreed to play nicely.

BEYOND MUSIC AND DOGS—MANY QUESTIONS

These stories of dogs and music are merely the starting place for our inquiry into the effect of the human soundscape on our canine companions. History shows that people, regardless of national identity, simply adore music. With its delicate balance of harmony, melody, and silence, music (in all its varied forms) is the most divinely wonderful organization of sound. Research shows that aside from entertaining, music also impacts the human nervous system, either arousing or soothing it. No wonder it is an integral part of every culture.

Many millions of music lovers are dog lovers, as well. So when we come to understand that many of the sonic effects of music also affect our pooches—be they mutts, shepherds, Labradoodles, or any of their five hundred-plus brethren breeds—it is cause for us to take notice.

Moreover, we know that an external periodic rhythm can affect the human heart rate, brainwaves, and rate of breath—speeding them up or slowing them down, depending on the pace of the beat. It may be news to us, though, that external rhythms also affect heart rates in our dogs. Given this recent discovery, what can we extrapolate about the effect of other man-made sounds—television, radio, answering machines, cell phones, construction, car alarms, helicopters? You and I know when we're overwhelmed—our minds and bodies let us know. But what about our dogs? Is that extreme salivation or restlessness just a characteristic of a particular breed, or is it actually a stress signal that we're failing to recognize?

SIGNS OF STRESS

Here are some subtle behaviors that you may not recognize as indications of an uncomfortable dog:

- lip-licking out of context
- yawning when dog is not relaxed
- looking away
- increased panting

Through a Dog's Ear is designed to initiate conversation and raise awareness about the impact of the sonic environment upon our canine companions. Many important questions come to mind:

- Does the human sonic environment support or destabilize a dog's well-being?

- What transpires with the compounded effect of modern urban living and the accompanying sounds of people?
- Is music simply noise to dogs? Or is the dog's unyielding bond to humans causing them to perceive music in a more human-like way?

This book is built around consideration of questions such as these. *Through a Dog's Ear* is a pioneering inquiry and, as such, may be a breeding ground for more questions. However, we believe there is great wisdom to be gained in the asking.

DO YOU HAVE A DOG AND SOUND OR MUSIC STORY TO SHARE?

As we continue to discover new questions and answers, we invite you to share your own observations about music and sound and dogs. Please contact us through our website, www.ThroughADogsEar.com.

DOGS AND HEARING

Just like our own auditory system, canine hearing is finely tuned. And just as with us, it can be an extremely important tool for both survival and communication—even more so for Fido. Despite obvious differences in ear structure, the process of hearing is the same in humans and dogs. Sound waves hit the cochlear (hearing) nerve, located in the inner ear, and then travel through the brain stem into the cerebral cortex. This is the area of the brain where both dogs and people process sound. A sophisticated hearing test called the Brain Auditory Evoked Response (BAER) reveals that the transmission pathways are the same across species. Veterinary neurologists often use the BAER process to test for deafness and for brain stem illnesses in dogs.

Although deafness can occur in dogs as they age (just like with people), many deaf dogs have a genetic defect that doesn't allow their hearing to develop correctly. This defect is often found in white or partially white dogs. If you suspect your dog is hearing impaired, try the following tests:[2]

- Call him or make a noise when he is sleeping
- Shake keys or a can of coins
- Squeak a toy behind your back
- Clap your hands loudly

If he does not respond to these stimuli, talk with your veterinarian about an ear examination and referral for the BAER. This test is the only way to know if one or both ears are affected.

Unfortunately, many dogs are euthanized because of their deafness, even though there are wonderful training programs and products available for the guardian of a deaf dog. It doesn't take hearing to be a loving companion.

While similarities exist between canine and human hearing, we also know that there are important differences. Humans hear sounds between 20–20,000 Hz. Dogs hear a much wider frequency range, especially in the higher pitches. The lowest frequencies canines hear are almost as low as with humans. In terms of the high end of frequency perception, it is at least twice as high as humans. Estimates vary from 40,000 Hz all the way up to 55,000 Hz—depending on the breed.[3] Maybe this is why many dogs have floppy ears—to cover a very sensitive auditory canal. Without these "ear" lids, perhaps they would be overwhelmed by too much sound, too much of the time. Sound is so important to dogs that their ears move constantly, like a radar dish, tuning in to sounds that we can't even perceive. (Can you imagine the ramifications for us if our ears moved like that? Big effect on sunglasses and iPods!)

Studies have shown that many common human behavioral and physiological issues may have an auditory component: attention and focus issues, anxiety, depression, and sensory integration challenges, for example. Is it possible these issues also apply to our dogs? After twenty years studying the often subtle, yet profound physiological and psychological impact of sound upon people, we're convinced our animals are as much at risk to sensory overwhelm as we are. Our dogs and cats just don't know how to express their stress in a way we understand, and we haven't known what to look for.

THE NUTRIENTS OF SOUND

Dr. Alfred Tomatis, an ear, nose, and throat surgeon and sound therapy pioneer, ascertained that the primary function of the human ear is to take the energy of sound waves and charge the cerebral cortex of the brain. As noted in the introduction, Dr. Tomatis also believed sound to be an important sensory nutrient for the nervous system.[4]

DR. SOUND: ALFRED TOMATIS

When we think about the effect of sound on living things, regardless of their leg count, Dr. Tomatis must be acknowledged as the premier sound researcher of the twentieth century. A few of his most interesting discoveries that inform this book include:

- The primary function of the ear is to convert sound waves to electrochemical impulses that charge the neocortex of the brain.
- Sound is a nutrient; we can either charge or discharge the nervous system by the sounds we take in through both air and bone conduction.
- There is a distinction between hearing and listening.
- Communication is a process that begins in utero.

For further information, visit www.Tomatis.com.

As with sun, water, or food, too much of a good thing can be harmful, sometimes even disastrously so. According to Dr. Tomatis, the same holds true with sound. There is no such thing as a sound-related illness in people. However, research has shown that constant noise diminishes immune and nervous system function. Studies conducted in Toronto, Canada, and Bombay, India, found that the anxiety produced by a perceived loss of control over personal environments, including noise, caused over-stressed bodies to become fertile ground for disease.[5] Additional research confirms that people exposed to chronic noise have significantly higher levels of the body's stress hormones, adrenaline and cortisol. According to the World Health Organization, the "most disturbing thing about noise is that you are being exposed to this reaction all the time." The long-term effect of constant stress hormones is that "it can literally corrode the body, eating away at blood vessels and other organs and predisposing a person to other medical woes."[6]

People who have dogs recognize that their own health and emotional states affect their canine companions, and vice versa. Given the extraordinary symbiotic relationship between humans and dogs—12,000 years in the making[7]—is it possible that the same noise pollution that we endure is also suffered, perhaps even more so, by our dogs? Given our dogs' increased sensitivity to sound and lack of control over their environment, perhaps human sound has a greater effect upon our dog pals than we ever imagined. The canine stress response is hard-wired, just like ours; one can only imagine what effect such constant adrenaline and cortisol release might be having on our dogs' minds and bodies.

SECOND-HAND SOUND

Since the 1970s, the Monks of New Skete have lived as a community in Cambridge, New York. They support themselves by breeding, raising, and training dogs at their monastery.

In *How to be Your Dog's Best Friend,* the monks tell a story that perfectly illustrates the mostly unexplored issue of sound and dogs:

> *Once, an Irish setter named Queenie was brought to us, quivering like a leaf. The harried owner wanted to leave her with us for observation. "She shakes like that all of the time," she explained. "I don't know if she can take our lifestyle." This comment inaugurated a discussion of the lifestyle at the dog's home. The woman described her family as "active" and "robust"—and, she added, "very noisy." Meanwhile, her three preschoolers were in the car in the parking lot, alternately laughing, screaming, and crying. When asked if she wanted the children to be in on the consultation, the woman exclaimed, "Oh no, they're too noisy. When they're around, Queenie shakes even more!"*
>
> *As we explored the family situation, it became clear that this dog had hardly any time to herself. Except for a five-hour stretch at night when she slept, the poor animal lived in a constant barrage of noise and racket. Orders and requests in this family, whether to the dog or*

to one another, were screamed or shouted. The television was the nerve center of the home and was on almost twenty-four hours a day, even if no one was watching it. When the family went out somewhere, the TV and radio were left blaring because they were afraid Queenie might become lonely and launch a spree of destruction. Furthermore, the home was situated on a busy highway, which lent its own noise to what the family produced.

However, Queenie's shaking had started only when she was six months old. The family had purchased the dog when she was two months old, and the animal was fine for about four months. But once the shakes started, they continued, and now Queenie was almost two. In all her time with these people, she enjoyed a few moments alone (even defecation was while on a leash).

After two days in our relatively quiet surroundings, she stopped shaking. The problem did not appear to be genetic, nor did it seem to stem from any kind of high-strung nervousness. Trained in a park obedience program, she responded to normally spoken commands and even to whispered instructions. When with us, she seemed to enjoy herself thoroughly. She entertained herself by tossing balls, by sprinting, and by relating to her canine neighbors in our kennels. When the owners came to pick her up, they could not believe the transformation.[8]

This story embodies every one of the elements pertaining to sound as a stimulant for the nervous system. Queenie was completely over-stimulated, with no time for integration and reorganization. While the nervous systems of her human guardians could apparently handle this kind of chaotic sonic environment, clearly Queenie's could not. Perhaps people have a greater tolerance to over-stimulation, but such chaos will affect even the strongest nervous system over time. The deleterious effect of long-term stress on immune function is widely researched and documented.

WHAT ABOUT PETEY?

At the beginning of this chapter, we told a humorous and true story about a pianist, two dogs, and a parrot. Lisa played a composition by Greig, Willie howled, Petey yelped, and the parrot shrieked. What was that all about?

Lisa produces what she perceives to be beautiful sound on the piano. Willie, the Dalmatian, makes an aesthetic judgment that he likes this music and decides to *sing* along. Petey, the little dog, is confused, perhaps annoyed, or maybe frightened by Willie's braying—so Petey barks at the bigger dog, hoping he'll stop. To top it off, the parrot is possibly so bothered by the cacophony of sound that all he can do is rant at Petey, literally telling him to *shut up!* Why was the bird so adamant? Maybe the parrot just wanted to hear the music without the barking. Maybe the parrot was so confused by all the conflicting noises that he was getting a headache.

Maybe the parrot just didn't like Petey. We will never know exactly what was going on in that little head of his.

What the story does illustrate, however, is the effect of too much stimulus in the environment. It also reveals how each being—human, big dog, little dog, or bird—has a different tolerance to the same sensory input. Lisa, for example, was probably amused by the whole affair—for a short time, anyway.

How often have you been in the position where others appear able to handle a particular sonic environment, but it really causes you a problem? In the upcoming chapter, we'll talk about why that might be.

CHAPTER 2

The Effect of Sound on the Inhabitants of Your Home

H ave you ever considered the human process of sensory input? We hear, see, feel, taste, or smell something, and countless neurons fire, signals rocket, lights sparkle, and buzzers buzz. The brain is working like it's the Fourth of July. Analyzing the sensory input, our brain tells us where to turn, how to react, and it allows us to identify the source of the stimulus. This happens every waking moment. Our sensory organs are our first alert system, designed to inform the brain about external and internal conditions.

So what about our canine companions? One can only begin to imagine the level of auditory stimulation our human soundscapes inflict upon a dog's psyche, day in and day out. Just think of all the input they receive. Indoors, dogs are exposed to telephones, cell phones, and computer whistles and beeps. There are various noise prompts from the dishwasher, garbage disposal, coffee machine, refrigerator, microwave, washing machine, and dryer. Getting a little noisy in here? Okay, let's step outside. Here we'll find helicopters, sirens, car horns, and burglar alarms, each of which is specifically designed to grab our attention. So we scurry back inside, where even more noise awaits us: alarm clocks, phone message machines, speaker phones, faxes, music players, video games, and TV entertainment centers with six-speaker surround-sound. How could this auditory environment not be a bit confusing to our canine companions, who operate on instinct and often stay home alone?

Consider the effect these same noises of modern life have upon you—and then how your disposition affects that of your furry companion. By this time, little Precious is reacting not just to the stimulation of the soundscape around her, but to your reactions to them as well.

To compound matters further, when it comes to sound, your dog may not comprehend cause and effect. *You* know about the disembodied voice coming from the plastic box we call an answering machine; *you* are amused when friends yell at the football game on TV when a touchdown is scored; and that smoke alarm—not to worry! *You* know that it's shrieking horribly and making everyone run around like crazy because of the shower steam coming from the bathroom. So what's the big deal? Nothing much—to us! Fido, on the other hand, doesn't understand what's going on at all. What he doesn't comprehend repeatedly imprints on his mind as *unresolved sensory input*. For humans, sights, sounds, and smells that don't compute translate into confusion of one degree or another, and the same is true for your canine companion.

SENSORY CONFUSION: THE COST OF OVER-STIMULATION

When people don't know what to do with irritating or emotionally draining sounds, they become agitated and confused—or they tune them out. Humans are lucky that way: we have an auditory mechanism within the middle ear that can diminish our perception of offending frequencies. In the guise of two tiny muscles,[1] this built-in compensatory mechanism is mostly a godsend. But there is a price to pay for tuning out sounds. Once we've blocked them out, it is hard to get back the perception of these frequencies . Given that sound is a nutrient for the nervous system, when we begin to auditorily shut the world out, we cut off a vital source of energy as important as food, water, or the sun.

What about our animal companions? When dogs (cats, horses, or birds) can't make sense of incoming sensory data, do they also become agitated and confused—or do they block out the noise, and thus become dumbed down? While there hasn't been enough research in this area to make a definitive claim, the anecdotal evidence points to the fact that animals react to sound precisely the same way as humans do. Author Temple Grandin, Ph.D., is uniquely positioned to explain why.

THE ANIMAL'S ORIENTING RESPONSE

In her marvelous book, *Animals in Translation: Using the Mysteries of Autism to Decode Animal Behavior,* Dr. Grandin draws on personal experience with autism—as well as her distinguished career as an animal scientist—to deliver an extraordinary message about how animals think, act, and feel.

About sound, Dr. Grandin says, "Any novel, high-pitched sounds will cause cattle to balk, because they activate the part of the animal's brain that responds to distress calls. An *intermittent* high-pitched sound is that much worse. Intermittent sounds will drive anyone crazy; they're much more upsetting than a constant, loud din, whether it's high-pitched or not. You can't relax, because you are waiting for the next sound. And you can't turn this response off, either, because intermittent sounds activate your *orienting response*. People aren't so aware of this response in themselves, but if you live around animals you know it well. Anytime an animal of any species hears a sudden sound, something they weren't expecting, they stop what they are doing and orient to the source of the sound."[2]

Dr. Grandin has witnessed the same response with pigs, horses, and humans—autistic or not. She concludes, "I think the orienting response is the beginning of consciousness, because the animal has to make a conscious decision about what to do about that sound. If he's a prey animal, should he run? If he is a predator, does he need to chase something?"

THE HUMAN'S ORIENTING RESPONSE

The effect of the *orienting response* on humans is also significant, and as mentioned by Temple Grandin, rarely acknowledged. We first came upon this basic neurological function while researching the numbing effect of fast-cut edits, zooms, pans, and sudden noises on TV and in films. Dr. Robert Kubey and fellow authors of the study, "Television Addiction is No Mere Metaphor," reported that the orienting response was discovered in 1927 by Ivan Pavlov who came to understand that "the orienting response is our instinctive visual or auditory reaction to any sudden or novel stimulus. It is part of our evolutionary heritage, a built-in sensitivity to movement and potential predatory threats."[3] Pavlov discovered that the orienting response causes our brains to become more alert, while causing the rest of our body to become quiet.

Building on Pavlov's discoveries, Dr. Annie Lang, of Indiana University, found that our heart rates decrease for four to six seconds after an orienting stimulus. This means that the entire orienting response takes at least four seconds. In many TV ads, music videos, and film action sequences, quick edits occur at the rate of one per second or faster. This quick-edit style triggers an over-activation of the orienting response, which consequently overloads the brain.

Dr. Kubey has found that on a physiological level, long sessions of over-stimulation create fatigue, dizziness, and nausea. On the other hand, even babies, at six- to eight-weeks-old, do everything they can to *watch* a TV and follow all the fast movement on the screen.

Temple Grandin's observation about the animal's orienting process is almost identical to Robert Kubey's study on people. Simply said, when an event attracts a two- or four-legged's attention, it takes a few moments for the animal to analyze and assess where it is in space and time.

In observing the behavior of dogs, any guardian recognizes the process when an animal is sizing up an orienting situation—ears perk up, nose twitches, and eyes are alert. For a moment, the body is completely still. Once it analyzes the sensory data, the dog is up and out at full speed. What happens, however, when sound stimuli come too quickly, or if the dog doesn't recognize the sounds it is hearing? Could it be that a dog's natural reactive process to a sound event gradually disappears with over-exposure? Could too much non-reciprocated stimulus lead to silent mental confusion? What might be the physiological effect of such confusion on an animal that is hard-wired to make snap decisions and react quickly?

INTERMITTENT SOUNDS AND LACK OF PATTERNS

It is fascinating when researchers of very different disciplines arrive at the same conclusion. Animal behaviorist Grandin speaks about intermittent sound being upsetting because you are waiting . . . waiting . . . for the next sound. This makes perfect sense from a psychoacoustic vantage point. Intermittent sounds are a perfect example of pattern identification—or more precisely, the lack of it. The brain is always looking for a pattern. Auditorily, this is called *active listening*—we are finely tuned, alert, and actively focused. But this is designed to be a temporary state, lasting only until we find the pattern in what we are hearing. At that time, the information processing slows into *passive hearing.* But when we can't find a pattern—when sounds are intermittent—our minds are not free to move on to other things that require our attention, and the whole perceptual system essentially starts to back up.

If we add the effects of intermittent sounds together with sensory confusion, over-stimulation, and an overwhelmed orienting response, a not-too-pretty picture begins to emerge. If we have difficulty defining where we are in space and time, life can get a bit mixed up. *Frustration, confusion,* and *hyper-reactivity* are terms usually used in reference to a child with a neurodevelopmental label. Could these behaviors also be the precursors to canine anxiety and all its manifestations?

Looking for answers to this puzzle, we move on to chapter 3, where we meet Malcolm Gamble and his adaptable dogs.

CHAPTER 3

Adaptable Dogs

W e've concluded that over-stimulation leads to sensory confusion, due to the inability either to process input as fast as it is arriving or to put the input in context. We know that the impact of over-stimulation (i.e., chronic sound stress) on the human nervous system can be debilitating. What about an animal's nervous system? Does Lassie respond the same way you or your children do? For the answer to this, we turn to Malcolm Gamble, a British researcher whose laborious work led him to publish "Sound and Its Significance for Laboratory Animals."

After an exhaustive review of 126 studies, Gamble states, "Available data confirms that exposure to sound can stress animals, and the results could still be apparent several weeks later." He discovered that very loud sounds make rats and mice more sensitive to all sounds later in life. Sounds tend to startle the animals, and consequently may reduce their activity. The reproductive aspects were also quite interesting: offspring of pregnant mice that were stressed with sound exhibited abnormal behavioral patterns.

Gamble continues by mentioning that several hormonal, blood, and reproductive measurements are disturbed by sounds above 80 decibels (dB), such as a garbage disposal, vacuum cleaner, or a busy city sidewalk. He concludes that in guinea pigs and cats, "Hearing damage is governed by the duration as well as the intensity of the sound and is irreversible." Gamble also states that different animals react to sound at different thresholds. But they all react to one degree or another.[1]

In his 1982 report, Malcolm Gamble spoke about various species, from mice to primates. He found that canines, however, were difficult to use for sound research because they reacted to the presence of the experimenters. Dogs rapidly adapted to the conditions of the sound experiment, with some variation. He noted, "The actual levels were dependent upon the reactivity of the central nervous system of *individual* animals." Put another way, some dogs (like people) are more sensitive than others. Some have a slow and steady nervous system—like a Mac Truck. Others are very finely tuned—like a Porsche.

SYMPATHETIC OVERDRIVE

What makes some dogs, and some people, so reactive to their environments, while others are seemingly unaffected? The cause can be found in the manner that incoming information is processed. Genetics, environment, and upbringing all have an influence on how we perceive the world around us. This holds true for animals and people alike.

The purpose of our senses—hearing, movement, touch, sight, smell, and taste—is first and foremost to determine if we are safe, to help us stay alive. The perception that danger is near engages our fight or flight response, which initiates a series of physical processes that will allow our bodies to stay and fight or to run away very quickly. It is our sympathetic nervous system that governs this response, and it knows instinctively what to do to get us out of danger. It quickly redirects blood away from routine functions such as digestion and sends it to the big muscles. Our brain focuses, our heart pounds, we experience the adrenalin rush. In a matter of seconds, our odds of survival have increased.

In modern times, however, our lives are so stressful, so over-stimulated, that we are causing our bodies to go into the fight or flight response continually, even though there is no imminent danger. The cumulative long-term effect of all the multi-tasking, deadlines at work, and running the kids from place to place can be an overwhelmed nervous system. Chronic over-stimulation is like being on high alert all the time. We call this common mind/body syndrome of perpetual fight or flight *sympathetic overdrive.*

In the non-natural sonic environment that both humans and dogs live in, we have so many noises and signals demanding our attention: Be alert! Wake-up! Coffee's ready! Cell phone's vibrating, landline's ringing, computer's dinging. Everything is now a sonic alert. The consequence of the over-stimulated sympathetic nervous system in people can be chronic illness. Of all family doctor visits, 60 to 90 percent are due to stress-related diseases.[2]

Does sympathetic overdrive similarly affect our animal companions? We emphatically believe that it does. Consider the environment animals were meant to live in—with sunlight, birds chirping, other animals, and room to run. That reality is a far piece from the seven hours of television noise in today's average American home.

While Malcolm Gamble's work showed us that some dogs have the ability to adapt to over-stimulating sound environments, many others do not do as well. For some dogs (and people), it is an unnatural sound circumstance with too much stimulation. Given that many of our dog friends spend time in bewildering physical environments—be they high-rise apartment buildings, enclosed workspaces, or the like—they have had to adapt *their* nervous systems to *our* human environmental sounds. To add to the challenge, dogs are often left alone for long stretches of the day or night. How are they able to deal with irritating or confusing sounds? Fortunately, when compared to primates, cats, rabbits, and mice, *dogs seem to be the most adaptable*. Does this adaptability mean we should stop worrying about our canines' sound environment? Absolutely not.

THE ACTION/REACTION RESPONSE

All animals, including two-leggeds, instinctively respond to sensory stimulation from the environment. A dog's auditory instinct triggers an action/reaction response. Interestingly enough, your dog's auditory recognition of sound events leads him to primal responses not so different than our own.

- Abrupt sounds = Be aware
- Abrasive sounds = Remove the sound source or self
- Comforting sounds = Get closer to them
- Familiar sounds = Not to worry
- Threatening sounds = Prepare to defend
- Frightening sounds = Retreat and regroup

OBIE AND RITA

My old English sheepdog, Obediah, used to come to my Hollywood office with me. In my entertainment company, performers were constantly coming in and out of our offices, mostly dressed in funny costumes—singing, dancing, and making a row. The phones rang off the hook, and it was quite an exciting place—at least for people.

At first, Obie seemed very interested in who entered the office and would jump up, bark once or twice, run over to sniff, and greet the interlopers. As the years went by, however, he didn't even lift his head, and eventually would spend most of

Obediah

the day in a quiet office down the hall. It wasn't that he had *seen it all*. Rather, I believe he just gave up trying to figure out who was coming and going, who to herd, and who was part of the pack. When he died of cancer at just eight-years-old, I wondered how keeping him with me in my fifth-floor, carpeted office had contributed to his declining health. Bringing him to work was certainly a better choice than leaving him home alone, I rationalized. But maybe neither choice was in his best interest.

About six years after I lost Obie, I moved to New York City and took a job running an exercise studio my fiancée owned. I would bring her exquisite Japanese Akita named Rita, whose story of being hit by a taxicab I told in the introduction of this book, to work with me. At 105 pounds, Rita was a formidable indoor watchdog. Her imposing presence was enough to discourage any foul play. But when we walked down Broadway, Rita would cower and anxiously pull on her leash to get inside, away from the traffic and chaos of the city street. Once we were inside the studio, she would do anything to squeeze under the small counter, away from public view.

Over time, I noticed the same thing with Rita that I'd seen with Obediah: two big, beautiful dogs in their prime, both spending their lives in public, highly-stimulating environments, and both doing everything they could to disappear. They were herding and hunting dogs and neither was doing the job they were bred for. Like Obie, Rita died when she was just eight-years-old—many years after her car accident—but still short of a full life.

Clearly, Obediah's and Rita's environments did not support their good health. —Joshua Leeds

In the next chapter, we'll search for the balance between the demands of our human world and the health of our four-legged friends.

CHAPTER 4

Ownership or Partnership?

Ten to twenty thousand years ago, wolves discovered the value of humans. Chances are, the animals weren't attracted to our music. It was something far more basic—our discarded food scraps were easy pickings.[1] Over time, wolves (that had evolved into large dogs) were put to work hunting, guarding, and herding. Small wolves became indoor pets. When their larger brethren eventually got a paw in the door, domestication took a big step forward. So now, here we are, all together inside human villages and homes.

However, the average twenty-first-century Western household is significantly different than the hovels of, say, 8000 BCE. In modern cities throughout the world, the human soundscape can be a cacophony of horns, helicopters, and boom boxes. Indoors, the bioacoustic effect of the human soundscape is more subtle, but nonetheless, often crazy-making in and of itself. Some dogs seemingly do okay with our rather bizarre sonic environments, but what about the ones who are more sensitive?

SO GLAD TO SEE YOU

When we consider a dog's optimal sound environment, we must take *instinct* into account. Instinct is one of the key concepts in our inquiry into dogs and sound. Interestingly, it has the same importance for people. In simple terms, instinct means *implanted by nature*. Highly tuned instinctive behavior is a hereditary reaction, hard-wired into the system, and unalterable through learned patterns of behavior.[2]

When a dog consistently can't identify the source of a sound, problems arise. (The same is true of people.) Imagine how many times in a day your dog cannot complete its natural reflexive process. If an animal doesn't know what is going on, the stifled reactive reflex ultimately manifests as anxiety or fright. This is the orienting response that we explored in chapter 2. Ever wonder why your dog is so glad to see you when you come home? Yes, Horatio the hound dog is happy to see you. And, perhaps your presence also provides a context for the noises he's hearing.

Yet even the context your presence supplies doesn't necessarily make problems go away. For example, we all know how nerve-wracking it can be to listen to the sound of a TV in the next room, when the sound is separated from the image. It can be random, chaotic, and irritating. When combined with the sound of your neighbor's loud stereo, the resulting turbulence, for some, might best be described as sonic hell. If this is the way it sounds and feels to humans, what must it be like for our dogs?

Because sound is so ubiquitous, we rarely consider the effect of our sounds on others—and we definitely expect our animals to simply groove to whatever sounds *we* happen to need at that moment. However, secondhand sound is like secondhand smoke—it has a bigger effect than we've ever imagined.

WELCOME TO *MY* HOME

What would happen if we adjusted our soundscape to suit our animals? At first, this appears to be an unusual concept. However, if we think of our animals as extra-sensitive indicators of unsafe conditions, perhaps we could create healthier environments for ourselves by tuning into the furrier perception of things.

Given the adaptability of dogs, we make the assumption that they can easily adjust to our environment. After all, they certainly want to. They just want to please us, be near us, and be loved by us. Perhaps a dog's flexible nature and ability to adapt is what creates such vulnerability to sensory overload.

Anyone who has been around a dog knows that canines have deep emotions, but that doesn't mean that they know how to interpret sensory confusion or chronic overwhelm. With a cumulative build-up, anxiety or other behavioral issues begin to manifest. Perhaps our doggy pals have been trying to communicate that something in *our* environment is not agreeing with *their* nervous systems. But unless we are quite astute, it is easy to overlook or misinterpret their signals of distress. Because our canine buddies can't consciously tell us that something may be wrong, we must develop the sensitivity to understand what they need.

However much we want to do the right thing for ourselves and our animals, the reality of life is that humans need to live in modern environments with all its trappings. We can't give it all up to live on a ranch in Wyoming because it would be best for our border collie. Still, when there are choices to be made, we can consider our dogs and, for example, choose soothing music at a tolerable volume. We may be doing ourselves a favor as well.

Our beloved animal companions, like Obediah and Rita, are with us unconditionally. They don't judge us for keeping them in our apartments or taking them to work. They don't care if we didn't get the promotion, or if we aren't wearing the latest fashions. They are truly our companions—walking life with us, no matter what. They are always there for us when we need connection, even when our human family or friends can't be with us.

OUR PATHS TOGETHER

I believe the human-animal bond goes beyond companionship. Animals are here to be our guides and teachers, and to help us on this journey called life. The most important lesson they teach us is to love without judgment. They view us as special people, whether or not the rest of the world agrees. Some would say I'm just anthropomorphizing—giving human qualities to an animal. But how many stories have we heard about a dog that wouldn't leave a sick child or grieving widower's side? And, in the days following 9/11, the dogs brought in as comfort to the rescue workers were as important as the search and rescue dogs.

Instead of giving human qualities to our animals, I recommend humans take on a few of these animal qualities. As a veterinarian, I cannot forget the experience of losing a dog to smoke inhalation. This beautiful, young airedale pulled his toddler companion out of a burning house. The child is alive today because of his dog. Am I anthropomorphizing when I say he acted as any firefighter would? I don't think so. Was it a coincidence that this particular dog came into this family's lives? I don't believe so. And would the airedale do it all over again? You bet he would.

—Susan Wagner

DEFINING OUR CANINE RELATIONSHIPS

Through a Dog's Ear is about context—the way we define our relationships with our animals. Curiously, this often mirrors our relationship to ourselves. When considering the optimum environment for our animals, important questions arise:

- Are we owners or partners? Do we simply own the animal and make all decisions based on what is good for us, or have we consented to a guardianship based on a more reciprocal relationship?

- Is the environment we wish to create for our animal companions really the environment we should be creating for ourselves?
- What can we learn from the challenges our animals face?

The answers to these questions will inform your decisions about your animals, and even your family. The following story is a wonderful illustration of a woman and her dog and *their* context of *partnership* versus *ownership*.

ANNIE AND HER HERO

Our friend Annie never had a dog as a child but always loved them. New York City was not the perfect place to begin life as a dog person, but at age forty-five, Annie felt it was time. She adopted the dream dog of her childhood, a golden retriever, who had been found in a parking lot in the Bronx without any identification. She named him Hero. He would come to change her life in ways both expected and unanticipated.

Annie cherished Hero's companionship and could hardly wait to get home after work and get outside with her new buddy. Morning and evening walks and forays to the fenced-in dog park were not enough. In order to take Hero out of the city on weekends to places where he could hike off-leash in the woods, Annie decided she would have to purchase a car. Soon, the weekends weren't

Annie Brody and Hero

enough either. The turning point came one night in the city after a glorious weekend in the country.

It was raining and they were in a taxi driving down Park Avenue. Annie noticed that Hero's perpetual grin was gone and that he seemed to have become depressed. She wondered what the problem was, so she crouched down and put her head right next to Hero's to see from his vantage point. All she saw were sharp angles and glass and metal squares of gray and black. They had just been in the countryside with lush fields and rolling hills and trees—lots of round edges and wonderful smells of nature. No wonder he was depressed.

Annie then realized that unconsciously, she was having the same depressed reaction to the city as Hero. Through many years of living surrounded by concrete and metal, she had learned to flip a switch and accept the unnaturalness of Manhattan as the price for her lifestyle. But once she allowed herself to see this metropolitan world through Hero's eyes—to imagine the smells he was experiencing and to hear the sounds of the city through his ears—it was dramatically different. She suddenly knew she needed to find a more natural way of living. Looking and listening from Hero's vantage point, Annie woke up to what she needed to do.

She quit her job, sold her apartment, and moved to six wooded acres upstate. In loving her canine companion, her "soul-dog," Annie chose to experience the human world from *his* perspective as a way to understand what he was feeling and thinking. In realizing the city environment wasn't good for Hero, she realized it wasn't good for her, either. Annie's deep companionship with her pooch provided the courage to chuck it all and move. Annie desired to build a partnership that was best for *both* of them, rather than merely assert ownership. She realized that the conscious choice was to think beyond how the dog should adapt to her life. How could she create a lifestyle that would be harmonious for human and animal?

Flash forward a few years. Instead of life in the fast lane, Annie now lives at the end of a country dirt road with two dogs and a cat. She runs weekend dog camps for city people and their canines and is the marketing director for a company that distributes a line of holistic, all-natural dog treats. She likes to say that her life has literally "gone to the dogs," and she's proud of it.

I asked Annie what time she wakes up in the morning. She told me six a.m., but that she doesn't get out of bed until six thirty. When I asked her why, she said, "You know, it's cold and dark outside and I have two warm dogs in bed with me. What's the rush?"

Annie's story is heartwarming, but in truth only a few of us are able to leave everything behind and move to a rural setting with our dogs. However, even if we remain living in town, we can follow Annie as far as the two very inspired decisions she made. The first was to look at the world from her dog's point of view, and the second was to recognize that the same environment that was affecting her dog was affecting her as well. By taking those two steps, we can begin to make changes—even if only incremental ones—that can improve the quality of life for both our animals and ourselves.

NATURE'S CYCLES

All animals are inherently tuned to nature's cycles. Days are light and nights dark. Summer is hot, winter's cold. There are sleep cycles, times for hunting, and times for playing. Regular migratory patterns mark the seasons. Each cycle has its own sound patterns and all animals know these identifiers—it is a natural and consistent sonic system.

Consequently, the ultimate, healthiest auditory surroundings for dogs would be those with a natural setting. A farm, ranch, large backyard—anywhere outside the bustle of the city would be best. In natural settings, sounds create harmony and balance because they fall within the parameters of a dog's *instinctual* process of sensory perception.

It would be nice if everybody who had a dog could provide them with the optimal sound environment of the country. Our dogs would be happier, healthier, and would live longer. So would we.

⁝

Most of us live in cities or suburbs. So how do we handle this? Our next chapter, "Thoroughly Modern Dogs," delves into ways we can create the best sonic sweet spot for Spot.

CHAPTER 5

Thoroughly Modern Dogs

Most of us will continue to live in cities and suburbs throughout our lives, and most of our canine companions will adapt. Can we, however, make urban life a bit easier for them? We hope we will have many dogs in our lifetime, and we want them to be with us as long as possible. So, the question is, what can we do for our canine companions if we do live in the city or the suburbs? We must learn to think in a different way about our environments.

A starting point would be to look at the human world from the point of view of our animal's *senses*. (As explained in the previous chapter, Annie did this quite literally with Hero.) Then we can begin to adjust our home environment accordingly. In many instances, a number of small changes can add up to a larger effect.[1]

SONIC INVENTORY

To begin, take a sonic inventory. Spend thirty minutes sitting quietly in one place with a notepad in your hand. Catalog the sounds you hear inside your home. Also note the dominant sounds coming from outside. Notice your dog's behavior. Notice your reactions as well. Does your animal actively notice many of the sounds? Are you surprised at your dog's lack of reaction? Does your dog overreact to sounds you take in stride?

After a half hour, total the number of sounds and rate them on a one to ten scale, with ten being the most disturbing and one the least noticeable. You may rate them in two columns if you like—one for your pooch and one for yourself.

This simple exercise can serve as the beginning of a new sound awareness. Noises that you didn't even notice before could be a source of anxiety for your dog. After assessing the sound environment, ask yourself if there is anything you can change. Can you alter your environment to be more harmonious for your canine? For those situations where change is impossible or at best minimal, later chapters will instruct you on how to use music to mask unwanted noise and achieve a calming environment.

While you are observing your dog, also notice how these sounds affect you. Does your home provide a peaceful space of comfort? Can you relax there, or is your home environment unnerving and chaotic? Remember, your animal may pick up and reflect your emotional and physical condition.

After you've taken a sonic inventory, determine if the sound environment has a noticeable effect on you and your dog. If you sense that it does, that your animal has an increased sensitivity to sound, take note of the following sound ideas for a nervous dog. These simple tips could be the starting point to creating a less abrasive household—beneficial to all.

SOUND IDEAS FOR A NERVOUS DOG (INSIDE A CITY OR COUNTRY HOME)

If you have an anxious dog, try these simple tips:

- Keep the volume of the radio and television at a level that can't be heard from another room.
- Avoid playing the radio and television at the same time.
- If you are not actively watching the television, or listening to the radio, turn them off.
- Reduce the noise from sound-producing appliances—turn down the volume on beepers and buzzers.
- Lower the ring on your cell phone, and have it play a soothing ring tone.
- Instead of yelling to people in other rooms, walk over and talk to them in a normal tone of voice.
- Don't slam doors and drawers; avoid clanging pots, pans, and dishes.
- If you become overly enthusiastic during television sporting events, put your dog in a calm place, or outside if possible.

HOME AWAY FROM HOME

A sonic inventory can be taken in the professional setting as well. If your dog goes to work with you, pay attention to the sounds he is being exposed to. You've probably become accustomed to loud co-workers, ringing phones, intercoms, and elevator sounds. While it is wonderful to have our dog pals with us at work, and often a much better scenario than leaving Rover alone all day, be sure it's really in his best interest to tag along. If you are in a high-energy environment, see what you can do to alleviate an onslaught of unnatural sensory stimuli.

Veterinarians, veterinary technicians, groomers, and kennel workers may want to participate in the following exercise.

Spend a few minutes actively tuning into the noise level surrounding the animals. You may be surprised to discover how often a dog or cat jumps when a cage door is slammed, the clippers are running, or the vacuum is sweeping up the hair. Are staff members yelling across the room? Is the intercom wailing? What type of environment are you expecting your patients to heal in?

Most veterinary offices play music that suits the staff; unfortunately, many don't consider the effect on their patients. A noisy kennel can easily compound the stress of a boarding animal already upset about separation from her guardian.

Finally, you may want to consider what effect an unhealthy sonic environment has on staff and work productivity. Does everyone seem cranky? Stop and listen. Creating an environment that supports well-being, rather than causing discord, is a cost-effective management tip.

UNDER-STIMULATION

A home with too many irregular, unrecognizable, or disturbing sounds can over-stimulate your dog's nervous system, as well as your own. Can you imagine being left alone all day and having to negate your instinctual reflex many times an hour? This would make you pretty aggravated, anxious, or frustrated. Best way to deal with it? Tune out. Now, imagine this situation day in and day out. It is not a healthy scenario.

Likewise, picture yourself in an environment where there is very little stimulation. What is your dog pal going to do? Read a book? For many dogs, life is either filled with too much stimulation or too little. (Yet another similarity they share with people.)

Although separation anxiety may be based in the fear of being alone or a manifestation of general anxiety, it can also be caused by boredom. Dogs are social animals—they enjoy being around other animals and humans. If they are alone, they can act out with destructive behaviors. If you spend time in the house with your canine companion, but never interact with him, it can have the same effect on him as being alone. Socialization requires interaction.

If you feel your dog is not enjoying enough companionship or stimulation, we recommend a wonderful book, *150 Activities for Bored Dogs* (see the Resources page). You can also consult a behavioral professional for safe toys and activities that will stimulate your dog's nervous system. When you are creative, there are fun ways to bring out the puppy in both of you.

UNDERSTANDING YOUR ANIMAL'S NEEDS

What is the solution to hyper- or hypo-stimulation? The first step is taking the time to understand your animal's needs. You might begin by recognizing your motivation for inviting Fido into your life in the first place.

Perhaps you acquired the dog so there would be someone to greet you when coming home to an empty house. Maybe you got this animal to help you exercise. Did you bring this animal into your life to provide protection or companionship for your kids? How will you compensate your canine for serving your needs? Understanding the basic sensory requirements of your dog is an appropriate reciprocal step. The payoff could be a longer, healthier dog's life.

SOUND AWARENESS FOR CITY DOG GUARDIANS

In addition to psychological aggravation, hearing loss is something to be aware of for both you and your animal. Sounds are measured in decibels (dB), and each 10 dB increase represents a tenfold increase in sound energy. Thus 90 dB is ten times noisier than 80 dB.

In human adults, 80 dB is the maximum sound intensity that will not produce hearing loss regardless of duration. In other words, no matter how long you listen to something at 80 dB, you do not have to worry about ear damage. Above 85 dB, you start playing with auditory fire. Inside the inner ear, irreparable cilia cell damage worsens with length of exposure and higher decibel levels.[2]

Your canine's inner ear works in exactly the same way yours does and has an even wider range of frequency. We've all seen our canine friends turn their heads as if to say, "Hear that?" We look around for the sound and remain clueless, while their orienting response has been triggered.

There is no reason to believe that canines are resistant to loud noises. A nearby jackhammer has the same effect on both species. It initiates the fight or flight response, which can manifest as the kind of panic Rita experienced when she heard the car backfire (see the introduction). In fact, some behaviorists believe that noise phobias are more likely to occur if the sound induces an instinctive fearful re-action. As you and your dog go for walks, be aware of the soundscape around you. Sonic awareness is no more than common sense. Avoid noisy construction sites or rush hour traffic. It is probably too much sensory data coming too fast—especially for highly reactive animals.

Remember, for both you and your canine, volume level and amount of exposure are key elements. We have to live in our modern culture, and hiding from it doesn't work very well. All aspects of our culture will show up wherever we are. As is the case for a martial artist, success comes with how we manage elements that come our way.

The following table shows the decibel levels of common noise environments.

HOUSEHOLD AND STREET SOUNDS[3]

NOISE . . . . . DECIBELS (dB)	
Watch ticking 20	Screaming child 90
Whisper 30	Subway platform 100
Average conversation. . . 40	Snowmobile 105
Quiet neighborhood street. 50	Symphony orchestra (playing very loudly) . . . 110
Dishwasher, microwave, blower on furnace 60	Power drill, chain saw . . 110
Alarm clock buzzer 70	Automobile horn 110
Blow dryer 70	Snow blower. 110
City traffic 70	Jackhammer 110
Noisy restaurant 70	Pneumatic drill 110
Garbage disposal, vacuum cleaner 80	Ambulance 130
Busy city sidewalk. 80	Jet engine at 100 ft . . . 130
Danger Zone	Gunshot 130
Battery-powered siren on toy ambulance. 90	Fire engine siren. 140
Lawn mower 90	Jet engine nearby. 140
	Boom cars. 145
	Helicopter. 150

TV AND RADIO

You may be tempted to leave on the radio, stereo, or television when your dog is home alone. This is not necessarily a bad idea, but you want to make sure that the resulting sounds are going to reduce your pup's anxiety, rather than make things worse.

In most cases, people hope to help the animal not feel too lonely while they're gone, or they may wish to provide some form of stimulation during long hours of isolation. These are good intentions. However, regarding TV, we believe that dogs and cats know the difference between a conversation their guardians are having with loved ones and the daytime soaps or game shows. (Do they really care who the heroine is sleeping with today, or if the returning champion survives new challenges?)

For the radio, you have the choice between music or talk radio. If you have a favorite radio station that you play while you are home, keep it tuned there while you are away.[4] If you choose to leave on a music station, we suggest finding a classical format. However, in tests conducted by Dr. Wagner, we ascertained that simple and slow classical music is even more effective than raucous crash-and-bang symphonies. (See chapter 7, "Breakthrough Research.") Consequently, CDs fitting this description may be most effective for calming and anxiety reduction.

MUSIC — WHAT CAN IT DO?

- Music can calm us and put us in an emotional space of safety. Our animals will entrain physiologically to the musical rhythms and psychologically to us. Entrain, in this context, means *to match*.
- Music reduces our heart rate and blood pressure, thereby providing an environment conducive to self-healing.

- Music can be a filter for unwanted sounds.
- Music is a vibration that is in line with our natural state of being.

For a continually updating list of recommended music and sound recordings, created specifically for canines, visit ThroughADogs Ear.com.

The best thing would be to play an intentionally selected CD rather than the uncontrollable play list of your local station—especially if you have a sensitive dog. Radio programming is driven by advertising dollars and the stations are looking to either stimulate or soothe their human listeners depending on the time of day and traffic patterns. Consequently, a wide array of classical music is delivered with specific intentions that might not fit what you are looking to accomplish for your pup.

The CD that accompanies this book contains selections from the *Through a Dog's Ear* CD Series. This music has been clinically demonstrated to calm canines and reduce anxiety. (See CD description, page 119.)

From a psychoacoustic point of view, one reason to leave a radio or TV on when you leave your dog alone is to create a filter that masks other irritating sounds. *Masking* is the process where one sound source essentially hides others within a similar frequency range. This can be beneficial, assuming that the sounds you do leave on do not simply add to the cacophony, irritation, or tune-out level of your pooch.

Whatever you do, don't leave on more than one sound source at the same time. This is a recipe for failure. Like it or not, the brain is hard wired to analyze *every* sound we hear. Sending too much data for too long will eventually degrade mental function. Too much of anything is not preferred. Sound balance is the goal. We may mean well when we leave a TV or radio blaring all day. However, imagine how you would feel at the end of a day if you were a captive listener with no way to change the channel or turn it off.

One solution is to have a timer on your radio, stereo, or TV. Let it play for an hour and then turn off. Too much repetition causes habituation and the effect may become meaningless.

There is a simple and quick check to determine your animal's relationship to the sound source. Where does your dog stay in proximity to the TV or radio? Is he close by or does he get as far away from it as possible? Learn to read his clues. Little things add up, positively or negatively. Your goal, as a conscious dog guardian, is to increase the positive effects and decrease non-beneficial influences as much as you can.

Intentional sonic environments may not be easy to create, especially in the city where there is so much random noise. However, through awareness and assessment, you can gradually figure out what to remove and what to add. It is a process that takes time. However, like the transition to a healthy diet, once the payoffs are observed, additional steps are not a burden—rather, they are a means to a desired end. In the case of your canine companion, the goal is increased well-being and decreased stress. So by trial and error, adding sound awareness to diet and exercise, you are building a program that will create a longer and better life.

In the next chapter, "Why Music Affects You and Your Canine Companion," we will explore intentional music as a mechanism for creating a healthy sonic environment.

CHAPTER 6

Why Music Affects You and Your Canine Companion

M usic can be perceived in many different ways. To people, music is a combination of tones, intervals, and rhythms with potential to evoke an emotional response. We have preferred styles (jazz, world, country, opera), favorite vocalists, and lyrics that often elicit treasured memories.

To dogs, however, music may just be another form of sound (perceived as noise?), that also contains fast or slow rhythms and high or low tones. There is no way to know exactly how a dog perceives form or emotional context in music. However, many of us have known animals that looked and acted as if they were truly enjoying music. Remember Willie, the Dalmation who loved Grieg? We have a friend whose cat had to be a reincarnated jazz piano player—he would hang around when our friend's band played, then walk across the piano keys as if to add to the music.

It appears that some animals really love music, while some others may have only a momentary fascination. Some canines appear to be oblivious. Regardless of preference or level of attention, we're learning from current research, including our own, that music provokes a neurological response in dogs similar to that of their guardians (see chapter 7). The natural psychoacoustic process of resonance, entrainment, and pattern identification takes place in our canine companions as well as in us.

Just as most people don't realize the effect of music on their own nervous systems, dogs don't understand the fact that their major body pulses (heart rate, brainwaves, and breath) are being manipulated by music. Truthfully, we don't know exactly how dogs perceive the wall of sound we call music. But we believe that one of the primary reasons that music is universally adored and incorporated into daily life is that it *plays* the neurological system of the listener—human or animal!

Given that aesthetic preference doesn't apply, Fido is not a hot, new market for pop or hip hop record companies. However, Dr. Deborah Wells, as noted earlier, discovered that heavy metal music (played by the band Metallica) caused canine agitation while classical music caused relaxation and sleep.[1]

We can't engage our dogs in a conversation about the distortion of heavy metal or the sonata form of classical music. But somehow, violins or piano solos have a different effect than screaming guitars and crashing cymbals. From a psychoacoustician's point of view, this differentiation falls under the aegis of *resonance*—the process whereby one vibration has an effect upon another. In other words, vibration "A" can change the frequency rate of vibration "B." Let's take a brief look at this important sonic phenomenon. It applies to all living things—including you and your doggy pal.

RESONANCE AND ENTRAINMENT

One important reason that sounds affect us is that all living beings require natural and periodic rhythms to live. Our brain waves, heartbeat, breath, and hormonal cycles all have a regular rhythm. Each of us is connected to the larger rhythms of the earth and solar system, as well. The sun always rises and sets, and spring always follows winter and precedes summer. Nature is made of cycles.

In fact, everything that moves in a cycle creates a pulsating rhythmic vibration. Frequency is the speed of a vibration and is measured in cycles per second—known as hertz (Hz). Through the process of resonance, one frequency can actually speed up or slow down another. Imagine that frequencies of sound can change the frequencies of our bodies. Calm frequencies help us become relaxed; chaotic frequencies make us frenzied and disordered. High frequencies tend to *charge* the nervous system; low frequencies tend to *discharge* the nervous system.

The same holds true with *entrainment*, the rhythmic aspect of resonance. External periodic rhythms affect the tempo of our heart rate and the speed of our brainwaves and breath. In general, fast rhythms excite and slow rhythms relax. External rhythms affect the tempo of our heart rate and the speed of our brainwaves and breath.

PATTERN IDENTIFICATION

Pattern identification is a third psychoacoustic technique worth explaining. Auditory pattern identification is a natural and analytical process of the brain. The brain uses pattern identification to determine the most appropriate expenditure of energy. The brain *always* seeks a pattern—it is an ecological function designed to preserve energy. Upon finding a pattern, the actual cerebral processing is moved from an *active* to *passive* category. Put another way, once the brain determines that it is safe, it delegates the remaining processing jobs to lower passive functions, thereby allowing the frontal cortex to be alert for new sensory input. On an auditory level, this process involves the shift from active listening to passive hearing. When a new sound is introduced, we are in active listening. Assuming we are able to identify a pattern, it is only a matter of time until this active state is downgraded to passive hearing.

Understanding auditory pattern identification allows us to adjust our environments so we find the right balance of stimulation (active) and relaxation (passive). Too much of either leads to imbalance that ultimately manifests in the mind or body.

Between resonance, entrainment, and pattern identification, sound can have a powerful effect on the human nervous system.

Until the studies of Wells and Wagner, we did not know if we were barking up the wrong tree in applying the same psychoacoustic principles to canines. What a surprise to find that dogs respond even more favorably to psychoacoustically designed classical music than to any other musical style.

MUSIC FOR DOGS AND PEOPLE

As we have explored the impact of sound on dogs, one point keeps surprising us: the nervous systems of our canine friends seem to be influenced by tone, rhythm, and patterns in somewhat the same manner as ours. What makes people sleepy, makes dogs sleepy; what irritates humans seems to agitate dogs. One could perhaps understand this if both guardian and animal were in the same room or house when the music was played, because in that case the dog might be reacting more to the human's vibe than the music. However, these results bear out even in animal shelters.

The CD within this book contains selections from the CD series, *Through a Dog's Ear: Music for Calming Your Canine Companion*.[2] This music is specifically designed to calm your dog and help abate behavioral issues. Additionally, included are tracks from the *Music for the Canine Household* series. This music is designed for human consumption, and clinically documented to have no deleterious effect on a sensitive canine nervous system. (Detailed information can be found on page 119.)

As noted earlier, *Through a Dog's Ear* CDs were extensively tested on more than 150 dogs in various environments. Of the four musical programs selected for use in these tests, one program had the greatest relaxation effect. A simplified solo piano at about 60 beats per minute seemed to be the right sonic formula when tested against even slightly faster, more complex solo, trio, or full orchestral classical compositions.

For the human heart, 50–70 beats per minute is considered to be the ideal relaxed heart rate, and the selection and arrangement of pieces on this particular CD adhere to this. Dogs responded to the music that was best for people. This is yet another indicator of the unique physiologic relationship that has formed between people and dogs. *They* were most profoundly influenced by music geared to *our* body tempos.

MUSIC FOR THE WILD ANIMAL KINGDOM

The effect of sound and music on animals is not limited to dogs. Music researcher Sue Raimond has found similar extraordinary results while playing harp for all kinds of wild animals, including wolves, elephants, and monkeys.

During 2004 and 2005, Sue played the harp twice for elephants at the San Diego Wild Animal Park. Sue was playing in a triangular protective "cage." Semba, an African female elephant weighing 4,600 pounds, freely meandered around Sue's enclosure. Semba had become quite jumpy since receiving puncture wounds and a

Sue Raimond with Koala Bear

chipped tusk from another elephant. Among other repercussions, she had become quite sensitive to noise.

When Sue began to play, Semba took on an aggressive posture. Throwing her big ears out, she trumpeted loudly with the pretense of charging. Sue says, "She was trying to be big, but she was actually really fearful."

As Sue continued to play, Semba's posture began to change. "You can tell the level of relaxation of any animal by their head, ear, and body position." With elephants, the position of their feet also tells much. Semba raised her back right foot and crossed it at her back left leg, below the knee, in a classic relaxation posture. As the minutes went by, Semba became even more comfortable and less afraid.

When Sue returned to play six months later, Semba came up to her quickly, as if remembering the first concert, and immediately put her trunk through the bars of the cage, trying to get as close as she could.

During this same performance in the African elephant barn, another elephant, a mother of a six-month-old baby, came over to look and smell. After a few moments, she went back to the other side of the enclosure and, with her trunk, pushed her 400-pound baby toward Sue and the harp. This is very unusual, as elephants usually keep their babies protectively behind them. The baby elephant's trunk came up and through the bars to sniff at Sue and her harp. After a few moments, the baby found a knob on one of the nearby bars, and spent the rest of the concert standing and playing with it with her trunk.

Part way through this last performance, Sue started to hear a very low rumble. She thought it was a large and heavy gate being pulled open. She then realized, however, that it was actually four other elephants, who were roaming free in their individual barn enclosure. They could smell and hear Sue, but not see her. The matriarch elephant began varying the pitch of the rumble and all the others followed with their sound. They were communicating through very low, subsonic vocalizations.

Later that day, in the Asian elephant barn, Sue set up her harp and played for Carol, an elephant with a history of depression and aggression. Unlike with other animals, Sue was able to look into Carol's eyes without fear of being perceived as aggressive, and she recalls, "pain etched her eyes." After a few minutes of harp music, Carol rested her head on the bars of Sue's enclosure and fell asleep. There was no more aggressive behavior. Carol remained relaxed for three days.

> We are privileged to include detailed information about the work of Sue Raimond, along with more of her wonderful music and animal stories, on our website, www.ThroughADogsEar.com.

In the next chapter, we will look at the astounding research of Drs. Wells and Wagner—pioneers in the study of how music affects the canine nervous system.

CHAPTER 7

Breakthrough Research

Recording the four classical CDs for dogs involved the same psychoacoustic principles used in recordings proven to provide deep human relaxation. Our belief is that there is a cost to the nervous and immune system for all sensory analysis, and when we are stressed or not well, we have little energy to spare. Yet, Dr. Alfred Tomatis also taught that sound is a vital and nutritive energy, important for healthy nervous system function.[1] Consequently, years have been spent trying to find ways to provide life-enhancing sound with a minimal depletion of the nervous system. As noted earlier, this concept is called simple sound.

When we first considered recording music for dogs, we had absolutely no idea if human brainwave states and heart rates corresponded in any way to that of the canine range. However, based on initial research, it seemed a good bet that what affected humans would have some kind of effect on dogs as well. We just did not know the extent.

From previous studies, we understood music did, in fact, have an effect on companion and farm animals. The value of *auditory enrichment* had been researched with a variety of species, including horses, cattle, birds, and primates. However, we were surprised to see that only one canine-specific study had been conducted.

DR. DEBORAH WELLS, BELFAST, IRELAND

In 2002, Belfast-based psychologist and animal behaviorist Deborah Wells undertook a research program to determine the influence of five types of auditory stimulation: human conversation, classical music, heavy metal music, pop music, and a silent control (no music at all). From Dr. Wells's study, we came to understand that classical music had a marked soothing effect on dogs in animal shelters when compared to the other types of auditory stimulation. In the discussion section of her published research, Dr. Wells stated, "Classical music resulted in dogs spending more of their time resting than any of the other experimental conditions of auditory stimulation. This type of music also resulted in a significantly lower level of barking. Research suggests that calming music may have a beneficial effect on humans, resulting in diminished agitation, improved mood and lower levels of stress. Although the specific effect of classical music on dogs remains unknown, the findings from this study suggest that it may, as in humans, have a calming influence." She concluded that heavy metal agitated the dogs, indicated by increased frequencies of standing and barking, and that neither human conversation nor pop music had any apparent effect on the dog's behaviors, perhaps due to habituation to radio exposure.

Dr. Wells stated, "Further work is still required to unravel the specific acoustic elements that dogs respond to."[2] That challenge inspired us to take our bioacoustic research where no one had gone before.

THE BIOACOUSTIC RESEARCH & DEVELOPMENT PROJECT

Understanding that some things about classical music were having an optimum effect on dogs, we endeavored to take Deborah Wells's work one step further. The purpose of our BioAcoustic Research & Development project was to investigate the effects of multiple types of classical music on the behavior of dogs in kennel and home environments. The music was chosen and arranged according to the principles of entrainment (beats per minute) and harmonic complexity (active listening versus passive hearing). We know that dogs have the same brain-wave patterns as humans. However, dogs' heart rates vary according to size; the larger the dog, the slower the heart rate. The tempos used in this project were based on an average-size dog.

We also recognized that domesticated animals possess more highly tuned hearing than people, yet we did not know if animal cerebral function would allow them to recognize sonic relationships (i.e., intervals, harmonies, and fast or slow external rhythms). In short, effectuating change in the human nervous system with sound and music is known, but what would be the result using the same principles on dogs?

After highly specific recordings were made, we created two pilot studies, involving more than 150 dogs. Between June 2004 and September 2005, these dogs were observed while listening to different combinations of the recordings Lisa Spector made for the project, as well as the control CDs, which consisted of non-psychoacoustically-arranged classical music.

TWO PILOT STUDIES

Pilot I. The purpose of Pilot I was to determine the efficacy of external rhythm and pattern identification on canines in the kennel and home environment. Four albums of psychoacoustically designed classical music were tested—two albums of solo piano at varying tempos and two albums of piano trios, also at varying tempos. The results suggest that all classical music doesn't have the same effect on behavior in dogs:

- In the kennel environment, over 70 percent of the dogs became calmer with the simplified, 50–60 beats per minute (bpm)—both solo piano and trio music.
- In the home environment, the solo piano at 50–60 bpm showed an average of 85 percent becoming calm, and over half the dogs went to sleep.

PILOT I SUMMARY

Instrumentation and tempo of the classical music can produce marked differences in results. Solo instruments, slower tempos, and less complex arrangements had a greater calming effect than faster selections with more complex harmonic and orchestral content.

Pilot II. The purpose of Pilot II was to determine if music arranged according to psychoacoustic principles would have an effect on specific anxiety issues in dogs, such as fear of separation, thunderstorms, and fireworks. Upon review of the data from Pilot I, it was determined that the simple and slow piano CD showed the most consistent results for calming dogs in both kennel and home environments. Because many guardians turn the radio on for their pets when they leave home or when a thunderstorm is approaching, another CD of standard classical music was chosen for comparison. This music was taken from the play list of a San Francisco classical radio station and was not psychoacoustically rearranged.

Ten dogs with anxiety were used in Pilot II. Their specific anxieties stemmed from the following:

- Other dogs or children
- Visitors in the home environment
- Thunderstorms

- Riding in the car
- Excessive need for attention—pawing at guardian
- Separation anxiety
- Fireworks

PILOT II SUMMARY

Results showed 70 percent of anxiety behaviors were reduced with psychoacoustically designed music, while 36 percent of anxiety behaviors were reduced with the non-psychoacoustic control CD. Both CDs calmed the dogs enough to make them lie down. However, it appears that the psychoacoustically designed music, with slower tempo and simpler arrangements and sounds, is more effective in reducing anxiety.

To view the complete research analysis of the BARD dog studies, visit www.ThroughADogsEar.com.

What is fascinating, from a psychoacoustician's viewpoint, is the fact that dogs were reacting in a similar manner to music that had been created for specific effects on people. In other words, dogs could be entrained, i.e., heart rate, brain waves, and breath slowed or speeded up when influenced by external rhythms, just as in people. It is also intriguing to note that the complexity of sound affected dogs as it does people: the more complexity in the music, the more energy required to decipher it. Likewise, the simpler the sound, the greater the relaxation response.

The fact that this simple pattern identification process had an effect on dogs with anxiety issues is even more startling for it suggests that dogs suffer from over-stimulation in the same way that people do. Stimulus is defined as "something that produces a temporary increase of physiological activity."[3]

We know from the extraordinary work of Dr. Alfred Tomatis that high-pitched (treble) sounds will *stimulate* and lower sounds (bass) *de-stimulate* the nervous system. (The first 80 percent of hearing cells in the inner ear process mid-high frequency tones. The remaining 20 percent of the cells process mid-low sounds. Dr. Tomatis discovered that if the ear is overwhelmed with too many low sounds, fatigue occurs and the brain does not receive the full benefit of the sonic energy. High sounds, on the other hand, create optimal stimulation.)[4]

Of the five CDs used in the combined studies, the single CD with the most startling results was one designed specifically for human calmness. This CD is the first in the *Through a Dog's Ear* series.

Entrainment—the process whereby our internal pulses will match a periodic rhythm—is easily observed in people who are tapping their toes and moving their heads to a rhythm. As we noted earlier, we have never witnessed a dog that pants or wags its tail to a beat. However, the results of these studies show that even without physical demonstration of rhythmic entrainment, the internal organs are still speeding up or slowing down to match external rhythmic stimuli. The ramifications of this are great. Our canine companions are totally impacted by the sonic landscapes in which we surround them — and ourselves.

ɞ

To this point, we have identified possible sonic causes of stress for both you and your animal companions. We have discussed sensory confusion, over-stimulation, fight or flight, sympathetic overdrive, and the orienting and action/reaction response. In the next chapter, we'll offer insights into your dog's behavior.

CHAPTER 8

About Your Dog's Behavior

Behavior medicine is one of the fastest growing areas in the veterinary profession. Statistics show that at least half of dog guardians talk about their animal's behavior with their family vet. It was not long ago that behavior issues weren't even discussed in veterinary colleges. Now, most schools have a behaviorist on staff, as well as behavior lectures and clinical training for veterinary students.

One of the most common behavior disorders is anxiety, whether brought about by thunderstorms, visitors into the home, separation from a guardian, or food-related aggression. Many signs that dogs exhibit are so subtle, the guardian may not even realize a problem exists. These can include lip-licking, yawning out of context, or looking away. Increased panting, whining, salivating, or hiding are more obvious clues that a pooch is uncomfortable. Worsening signs include pacing, trembling, urinating, defecating, digging, and chewing. Severe cases can have horrible consequences—dogs have been known to severely injure themselves trying to escape from crates, and have even thrown themselves out of windows.

We may miss anxiety in our canine companions if their behaviors are mild and are occurring at seemingly innocuous times. If the skies are sunny and your loud, obnoxious neighbor isn't anywhere close to your property, then why worry if Buddy is hiding under the dark table instead of taking his nap in his customary place next to you? The answer begins with classical conditioning.

Remember Pavlov's dog? He was one of the most famous experimental animals—every psychology student has learned about him. The stimulus, a bell, was sounded just before the dog was given food. After several similar sessions, the dog began salivating at the sound of the stimulus—he knew that food was on its way. (We like to joke that the true founder of behavioral sciences was a dog.)

As with Pavlov's subject, our canines can be classically conditioned—and so can we. Perhaps your heart beats faster and you salivate every time you drive by a favorite restaurant. Classical conditioning, however, can then progress to *generalization*. In the case of anxiety, the generalization occurs in a detrimental manner, where fears seem to escalate and are triggered by more and more events. Animals can become anxious over things that don't represent a threat, but are similar to the threat. For example, a dog that suffers from thunderstorm anxiety may become fearful of flashing lights or rumbling noises that we don't even notice. Dogs who have been abused may become fearful when approached by someone who looks similar to the person who hurt them. They are reacting just like Pavlov's dog, but to a stimulus that is slightly different from the one that originally caused fear. This is generalization. Canines learn and adapt very quickly, as we discovered from Malcolm Gamble's work. In negative circumstances, their adaptability becomes their Achilles' heel.

DIFFICULT BEGINNINGS

Beyond the chaotic soundscape, many dogs have had difficult beginnings. Even in the best of breeding circumstances, we may take puppies from their mothers at too young an age. There is a wealth of animal research, from mice to humans, that tells us the importance of a mother's touch.[1] Losing maternal contact at too early an age decreases an animal's or person's ability to handle stress, and can lead to physical and emotional disorders later in life.[2]

Let's also consider the abuses or challenges many animals have endured before coming into their current guardian's life. Unfortunately, puppy mills still exist. Many of these breeders keep animals in unhealthy and often cruel environments. Rescue groups and animal shelters, despite wonderful intentions, are frequently over capacity with six to eight million abandoned and unwanted animals.[3] Many of them were neglected, harmed, or left without food or water before being found.

Taking these difficult beginnings into account, anxiety and abnormal behaviors are quite understandable. It is generally accepted within the human psychotherapeutic community that adult psychological issues very often have their genesis in early unresolved childhood trauma. Why would we think that it would be any different for our four-legged companions?

Is it surprising that behavioral issues are on the rise when we look at modern society? Throughout this book, we have talked about the stressors both two- and four-legged creatures face today. If you recall, 60–90 percent of visits to family physicians have been linked to stress-related illnesses. These percentages look eerily similar to the 45–90 percent of veterinary visits for behavioral issues.[4] How do we help our canine friends adjust, when the real issue may be that the pace of modern life disconnects us all from our natural state of being?

INTEGRATIVE MEDICINE

Living with behavioral problems can be stressful for everybody involved, both dogs and people. Dealing with behavior issues usually takes patience, sometimes requires visits to professionals, and always involves time and effort working with the animals at home. There's no easy solution, no simple pill that will take care of the problem completely. If you find yourself feeling overwhelmed as you go through the healing process with your dog, don't be too hard on yourself. Rest assured that others have had to deal with the same experience, and they understand what your household is going through.

Getting to the underlying cause of your animal companion's behavior issues requires looking at the whole picture—life before your canine came to you, health problems such as chronic pain, the environment you live in, and the connection she has with you. The state of your body, mind, and spirit can and does affect your animal's. Using therapies that treat more than just the behavioral sign (in dogs) or symptom (in people) is very important. Approaching disorders as part of a larger picture is the definition of holistic, and combining the holistic approach with conventional medicine is called *integrative medicine,* which we believe to be effective and powerful.

Many types of complementary therapies are available for humans as well as animals: in addition to the sound and music possibilities explored in this book, there are movement modalities, botanically based therapies (herbs, aromatherapy, and flower essences),[5] and energy therapies (Healing Touch for Animals™, Reiki, Reconnective Healing™). Music is also a type of energy therapy, because its basis is the vibration of sound waves.

Quantum physics has taught us that every thing that exists is made of energy, including living beings. A profound, Nobel Prize–winning study conducted by Brian Josephson showed that tiny particles that make up our bodies are actually waves of energy. There's nothing solid about us—we just appear that way. Just as music entrains our brain waves and heart rate, our own natural vibration entrains people and animals around us.

As you can see, wonderful healing methods are available to you and your animal companion. (We have listed many of these in the resources section.) If you find you need professional help in treating a behavioral problem, you might consider seeking out a veterinarian who supports an integrative approach.

RESPECT — SOMETHING EVERY BEING DESIRES

Some behavioral professionals may appear to use a positive approach, but make sure you know what's happening behind the scenes. There are no requirements for dog trainers, nor are they licensed, although voluntary certification groups do exist. (See "Behavior" in Resources.)

The most important thing to remember in training your dog, or in hiring a trainer, is the word "positive." Reward-based training is effective. Treating anxiety or fear with more anxiety and fear doesn't make sense. Punishment-based training techniques have been shown to be ineffective and can create *more* fear and anxiety. If you, or your trainer, have used painful or fear-based methods in the past, you are not alone. I've certainly given my share of incorrect advice. However, the behavioral and training communities have come a long way and continue to evolve. I highly recommend supporting those individuals who advance reward-based training.

> Our canine companions are just like us. Would you rather receive praise for doing something well, or get criticized each time you make a mistake? Respect is something every being desires.
>
> —S.W.

SOUND HELP IS ON THE WAY

Sound is a key component to creating a healthy environment for guardians and animal companions alike. We weren't created in the middle of a big city; we evolved from natural surroundings. Take a few minutes to listen to nature. Birds are singing beautiful melodies in the morning, and the insects take over the symphony at night.

These sounds are part of the grand design for our world. Research indicates that the frequency most conducive to growing plants is the same frequency at which birds chirp.[6] This is no coincidence. As human beings capable of entraining and being entrained, we have to ask what our part is in Earth's musical score.

Although we may enjoy pondering the cosmic sound implications for humanity, nothing brings us back to earth like coming home to find the new couch chewed to pieces, or a *present* on the Persian rug. Why are sound and music so important in addressing these behavioral issues with our canine companions? Sound awareness and music therapy can calm our beloved dogs. Where calm and peace exist, fear will not.

🦴

In the following chapter, we explore the use of music and sound for some specific canine behavioral issues, including separation anxiety, aggression, thunderstorm anxiety, and excitement with visitors.

CHAPTER 9

Using Music and Sound for Behavioral Issues

A sonic approach to anxiety starts with recognizing the noise level in your home. Any clatter that suddenly gets an animal's attention may also create stress, whether it is a loud buzz from the clothes dryer or the slamming of the front door. We don't need to recreate the atmosphere of a library, but it is helpful to recognize the intensity of the sounds within and outside your home.

If there are noises that you have no control over, calming music can help. For example, if you live in an urban environment, playing the enclosed psychoacoustically designed CD for your canine during the honking horns of rush hour can certainly help ease the stress. (See "About the Enclosed Starter CD," page 119.) It's not necessary to play the music loudly, because the relaxation effect comes from passive listening. The hearing nerve is a conduit to the rest of the body, which will respond in kind.

IMPORTANT INFORMATION BEFORE USING MUSIC

There are some common reasons for using music to calm your anxious canine. Before getting started, it's very important to review a significant behavioral concept. Generalization happens when the animal (or person) learns to be afraid of something similar to the original source or cause of fear. It also occurs when they associate fear with something that has occurred during a stressful time. It can also be linked to the place where a stressful event occurred. For example, your canine may now be afraid to stay in your home, because that's where she was when a horrible storm hit.

Behaviorists tell us that the key to modifying any fear-based behavior is to create a situation that lessens fear. That might seem like common sense to you, but here's the catch. It's not whether *you* think it's a peaceful situation, it's *how your dog is feeling* that matters. So, you may put on the enlcosed music CD, feel calmer yourself, and think that your dog is going to settle down as well. If her anxiety is so severe, however, that the music is not enough, she may now associate the music with her fear. When you play it the next time you work with her behavior, the music makes her anxiety worse.

Here are guidelines for you to follow to ensure that your canine creates positive association with the music you're playing: Play calming music first when your dog is not experiencing anxiety. This will allow her to associate the calming music with a positive state of being. Once you have done this, you can proceed to using it in anxious situations. If the music doesn't keep her calm, stop and use it several more times when she is not fearful. Also, take time to learn what behaviors your dog shows when she is fearful. Don't hesitate to ask an animal professional for help in distinguishing these behaviors. Is she panting, whining, restless, or pawing at you? These are subtle signs you might miss if you're not paying attention. It's much easier to spot anxiety when your dog is throwing herself at the door as you are trying to leave.

No matter the behavior you are working on, it's important that your canine achieves relaxation and a sense of safety. If the music relaxes her to the point that all of her fearful behaviors are gone, proceed. If not, her anxiety may be too severe for music alone to help. Enlist a positive trainer or behaviorist to assist you. With a combination of a caring professional, music, and integrative modalities, you and your beloved canine will be supported through the process of addressing behavioral issues.

Finally, we'd like to expand on the concept of being worried. As we have explained, we are all made of energy. The human-animal bond is also based in energy. If you are constantly anxious about your dog's behavior, you will create even more anxiety for her. If you believe that nothing will help and that your lives are doomed to fear and anxiety, then this will only intensify the current situation. A truly holistic approach to behavioral "dis-eases" includes the human guardian's feelings. Do whatever you need to reduce *your* stress. Your balanced state of mind will greatly impact everything you are doing to help your canine companion. The better you take care of yourself, the healthier your canine household will be. This is the heart of a symbiotic relationship—helping each other.

SEPARATION ANXIETY

Music can be extremely useful in cases of separation anxiety. We recommend putting on *Music to Calm Your Canine Companion* twenty minutes before you leave, so that your dog has plenty of time for the entrainment to take effect. Set the volume at a fairly low level, but high enough so it serves to mask disturbing external sounds. Using it as part of a desensitization program makes perfect sense. Once your dog is relaxed, leave for a very short time—two or three minutes at first. Don't make a fuss over leaving—you want your dog to remain peaceful and quiet. The music should keep your canine calm for that period of time. Gradually increase the time you are gone. Your behaviorist may have other exercises for you, so ask if the music can be added to the protocol.

If you are leaving your dog alone for an extended period of time and have a CD player that plays multiple CDs, load it up with calming music. You can also put the CD player on repeat. Given that every being is different, try different CDs and time periods and observe what seems to work. We do not believe you have to be concerned with overdosing your animal with beautiful and peaceful music; just make sure it falls into the category of simple sound. (See pages 12 and 82.)

AGGRESSION

While it may seem logical that aggressive behavior is driven by dominance, experts believe it can be tied to fear.[1] When aggression is involved, consulting a veterinarian, behaviorist, or trainer is imperative. Choose a professional that uses only positive, reward-based methods, so your canine's fear is not intensified. You may also consider adding an energy practitioner to the team.

Reducing anxiety is very helpful when aggression and fear are concerned. Ask your animal professional if *Music to Calm Your Canine Companion* is appropriate for your dog's treatment plan. If so, play the music when your dog is relaxing inside or outside the house. Keep the CD on for twenty minutes to an hour; this can be done as often as your schedule allows. Listening to calming music can help *you* through this difficult situation as well.

THUNDERSTORM ANXIETY

Anxiety caused by storms can be one of the trickiest to treat. Animals have an instinctive ability to sense changes in the weather, especially severe ones. Prior to the tsunami of 2004, animals and birds were seen heading for higher ground long before the disaster struck.

Calming medications are often prescribed for storm-related anxiety. While they do help, they often don't take effect for thirty to forty minutes, and the storm may be over by then. Music therapy is a wonderful tool because entrainment happens so quickly—often within five minutes. If the weather forecast calls for storms, have the CD ready in the player. Your dog may have a location in your home he goes to during a storm, a place where he feels safer. It's important to allow him that safety, so a portable machine may be necessary. If the music is not enough to keep him completely calm, working with a behaviorist may be called for.

FIREWORKS

Many dogs are very fearful of fireworks. Calming music can be a perfect solution, because we usually know when the fireworks will occur. If possible, go to the basement or the room farthest away from outside sounds. You may need a portable audio device. Put the music on at least twenty minutes before the fireworks start. It will help calm your dog and also mask the unwanted explosive noise.

EXCITEMENT WITH VISITORS

Your behavioral professional has many excellent training techniques regarding visitors coming into the home. Having a 5-pound Yorkie jumping up and down isn't as dangerous as an 80-pound Labrador knocking Grandma over. Vivacious dogs are like a big family—always *so* glad to see you! We want to keep that happiness for our canines, but without the stress of a hospital run for our visitors.

The good news about this excitement dilemma is that it's easy to work on *before* Grandma comes over. You may want to have practice runs with your friends. The key to success is control over your dog, and one of the best ways to achieve this is to keep him calm.

Calming music can be put on twenty minutes before your guest arrives, and should help you with the obedience behaviors you will want to initiate. Sitting and staying are so much easier for your dog when he's relaxed. Have patience; it may take some practice.

HOUSE GUESTS

Dogs and people are similar in that most of us rely on our daily routine. Even house guests who are fun to be around can create a bit of stress. You can play calming music for an hour everyday to help your dog (and you) relax. You can also use *Music for the Canine Household* anytime during the visit to create an uplifting sound environment for you and your guests, yet still provide a positive experience for your dog. (See page 108.)

STRESSFUL TIMES FOR THE HUMANS IN THE FAMILY

Life is not without challenges. Severe or chronic illness, employment issues, financial burdens, or the death of a friend or family member can create enormous stress. Animals in the household are affected as well. Play calming music as often as you can during these difficult times. If you are going at a hectic pace, even ten minutes of music therapy can support your animal's well-being.

BOARDING

Many modern boarding facilities offer some of the comforts of home—comfy furniture, natural lighting, and play time with other dogs. Even kennels that have been in existence for many years may have a sound system, or an area in which a portable audio device can be played safely.

Ask your boarding professionals to play calming music for your dog while she is in their care. By association alone, this will help your dog feel a sense of familiarity with the sonic environment, at the very least.

DRIVING WITH YOUR DOG

Riding in the car can be very stressful for many dogs, and very exciting for others. In either case, this can create anxiety for the driver. You may be concerned about your dog barking, excessively panting, jumping up and down (even in a kennel), or running from window to window. A nauseated, motion sick dog can also be a huge distraction.

If your dog is not the perfect passenger, we suggest that *prior* to getting in the car she listens to twenty minutes of *Music to Calm Your Canine Companion*. [Please note: Do not drive while listening to the *Calm Your Canine Companion* CD. It may make you drowsy or cause you to fall asleep.]

Once you are on the road, play the CD *Music for Driving with Your Dog*. Make sure to always start at the beginning of the CD. These tracks are designed to keep you focused, while calming your canine. The piano music intentionally begins with softer, simpler pieces to relax your dog. The second half of the CD is more active, designed to keep the driver alert. Remember, for optimal results with your pooch, we recommend starting at the beginning of the Driving CD whenever you get back in the car to drive again.

Music for Driving is part of the *Music for the Canine Household* series. Further information is available at ThroughADogsEar.com.

MUSIC AND MEDICAL CARE: RECOVERY FROM ILLNESS OR SURGERY

Whether it be trauma, illness, or surgery, your animal's optimal recovery requires she be calm and rested. Modern veterinary medicine offers excellent pain management, but your animal may still have trouble resting. Calming music is a safe way to help your companion heal quickly. It doesn't have to be played continuously to achieve results. We recommend one hour of music, two to three times a day. If your animal has to endure a stressful situation, such as a bandage change, play the music prior to (thirty minutes is best) and during the procedure.

EUTHANASIA AND HOSPICE

Anyone who has ever lost a beloved animal companion knows how difficult it can be. While some animals die without suffering at home, most pass peacefully because their guardians have made the compassionate decision of euthanasia. Despite knowing it is the best thing for our animals, the time surrounding euthanasia or hospice care is emotionally draining. If your veterinarian is performing the euthanasia at home, we suggest playing *Calm Your*

Canine Companion for thirty minutes before he or she arrives. If you are taking your animal into the clinic, ask your vet if you can play this music for your companion prior to the euthanasia. It can help both of you through the transition.

ANGEL'S WINGS

Regarding the use of calming music for dogs, one of the most profound stories we have received concerns a wild dog named Angel. White and fluffy, Angel was born near a central Ohio farm owned by a kind woman named Paula. Angel was one of several puppies from a feral litter. All of her siblings had run away or been caught by humans, but Angel had out-smarted them all and learned how to survive well on her own. Paula and her friend Peggy, a seasoned animal rescuer, would watch her from a distance. Whenever they tried to get near her, Angel would dart away.

Soon Angel became braver and braver. She was spreading her wings and exploring her domain. Unfortunately, that domain included a busy country road. Paula and Peggy's hearts would stop when they spotted her crossing it. They knew they were going to have to tame this free spirit, or a disaster was going to occur.

Eventually Angel was coaxed into an enclosure on Paula's property. Each time they tried to come close to her, however, Angel became extremely fearful. They used the *Calm Your Canine Companion* CD everyday and stayed at a distance, allowing Angel to feel safe and secure. With time, they were able to gently approach her. The day Paula could finally pet Angel was a joyous occasion indeed. Now obedience training could begin, and Angel could fly safely.

In our next chapter, we'll look at the ways people and dogs can use sound to improve everyone's well-being.

CHAPTER 10

Living a Better Life Together

One of the most exciting elements of our explorations into psychoacoustics and the effect of sound and music on canines has been the realization that we now have a tool that humans and animals can use together for improving their well-being.

MUSIC AS ENERGY THERAPY

Music is a vibration that influences all energy fields—people, animals, and plants. It entrains with our brain and heart rhythms and with your dog's brain and heart rhythms in basically identical ways.

When it comes to psychoacoustically designed soundtracks, musical taste is not important. The effects of the music are passive, caused by the physiologic and energetic effects of the vibrations. Within a few minutes, your body, mind, and spirit will know something has shifted. So will the body, mind, and spirit of your canine friend. You may see your dog take a deep breath, lick his lips, yawn, or stretch. These are all evidence of relaxation and a clearing of his energy field. Likewise, your heart rate will decrease and your brain waves will shift to a slower frequency.

We are particularly excited about using music for service dogs that help their guardians achieve independence. Therapy dogs, like those who visit nursing homes or work with children with disabilities, will also benefit from music. These animals work so hard, their orienting response is always activated. Being continually in action can lead to physical and emotional stress. Music therapy offers a perfect opportunity for these beloved heroes. The guardians of helping canines also have their share of stresses. What a wonderful way to end the day—companions who take such good care of each other truly relaxing together.

DON'T FORGET TO MOVE!

While relaxing and listening to calming music is a wonderful way for guardian and canine to be together, it's not the only way. Both species require movement to stay healthy. Being sedentary leads to physical problems, whether you are two-legged or four-legged. What better way to get healthy than a walk in the park. You and your dog will receive the benefits of both physical activity and being in nature's harmonious energy field.

If your dog suffers from any type of anxiety, physical activity is extremely valuable. Research in humans has shown that aerobic

exercise helps with many mental health issues,[1] and animal behaviorists tell us it's equally important in dogs. You don't have
to become a marathon runner to help your anxious canine. Any
activity that increases his heart rate and is joyful for you both
is acceptable. Be sure to consult with your veterinarian on the
types of activity your canine can physically handle.   —S. W.

DOG- AND PEOPLE-FRIENDLY MUSIC

When we began to develop music for canines with Lisa Spector,
we referred to the research done by Deborah Wells in Ireland. Dr.
Wells showed that dogs preferred classical music to pop or rock 'n'
roll, but she did not evaluate varying types of classical music. As
we know, there is a world of difference within the classical genre.
Some music may be heavenly peaceful and others can be every bit
as frantic or distorted as heavy-metal rock. Therefore, we combined
our expertise in psychoacoustics and canine physiology, along with
Lisa Spector's extraordinary familiarity with the classical repertoire,
to develop four separate album concepts. Our goal was to discover
the effect of differing levels of complexity and changes in tempo.
This led to long hours in the studio for rehearsals, psychoacoustic
rearranging, recording, sequencing, and editing.

When we tested the music, it confirmed Dr. Wells' findings that
dogs show differences in sensitivity to music, just like humans
do. We believe that the behaviors we were witnessing in canines
were because their nervous and cardiovascular systems were

entraining to the music. This was quite a fascinating finding. The most profound calming effect was seen with the psychoacoustically designed, slow, simple piano music. We had indeed created industrial-strength musical medicine.

Calming is certainly desirable when our canine companions have anxiety disorders or are under physical and emotional stress. It's also indicated for humans in the same circumstances. However, what about a canine household that doesn't have anxiety concerns, or for those times in which calming isn't needed? What about everyday life, and the effortless enjoyment of music?

What our research revealed is that psychoacoustically designed classical music was always dog-friendly—meaning it did not exacerbate or increase behavioral anxiety. We discovered this by analyzing the behaviors that *weren't* there, along with the ones that were. While the more complicated compositions and sequences didn't calm dogs as much as simplified, slow piano music, it didn't agitate them either. They didn't pant more or become restless. In the home studies, the dogs didn't bolt out of the room. Instead, they were content to stay with their guardians while the music was playing. In other words, this more complex music may be appropriate for human consumption without a deleterious effect on sensitive canine nervous systems. We call this series *Music for the Canine Household.*

What does *Canine Household* music mean for our sonic environments? Our clinical testing shows that humans can enjoy uplifting music and know that their canines aren't going to be negatively affected. If we live in an area with street noise or other pervading sonic issues, we can put music on that allows us to function well while creating a filter that masks irritating sound. This creates a healthier sonic environment for the entire canine household. When experimenting with music, pay attention to your dog's behavior while you are listening. Most importantly, make sure Rover is able to leave the room if the sounds make him uncomfortable.

FUTURE RESEARCH

In the future, perhaps we will be able to test the effect of the Beatles, John Coltrane's jazz, and the twentieth century music of Stravinsky and Schoenberg. Based on what we have seen, however, simple arrangements, light orchestration, and slower tempos seem to be the key for canine calming and anxiety reduction. The style of music may ultimately not be the primary component, rather the regulation of auditory data. The less sensory data received, the less processing power required. Consequently, relaxation becomes a predictable result.

As further research is done on the effect of music on dogs and their humans, we will not be surprised to see soundtracks developed for many specific applications. These could include more detailed levels of anxiety and pain reduction, as well as music to assist in alertness and training.

WHAT ABOUT YOUR CANINE'S KITTY COMPANION?

Many people have asked us about using music with cats. After all, dog guardians can also be cat lovers. Even though there are cats who don't want to share their house (and we know it's *their* house) with a canine, and there are some dogs that would rather have kitty for lunch, we believe this is a rare occurrence. When a dog is introduced to a cat household, it is the feline that usually takes the upper paw. One good swipe on puppy's nose sets all the ground rules.

Our music was tested in many households with cats. Some stayed around and relaxed, others simply walked away. None appeared agitated nor took it out on their pooches. Wonderful research has been done on environmental enrichment in felines as a way to help them deal with stress.[2] Some work has also been done in the area of music. As we discover more, we suspect we'll find that kitty requires a faster tempo and more complicated orchestrations. Heck, cats get bored easily. That's one of the things we love most about felines—they have *catittude!*   —S.W.

꘎

In our final chapter, we summarize the process of becoming a sound-aware dog guardian and provide an overview of the interconnectedness of all things.

CHAPTER 11

Interconnected

Through *a Dog's Ear* advances the concept of conscious animal guardianship. We have asked you to consider the possibility that simple modification of your sound environment might make a big difference in your dog's life. We have asked you to become sound-aware and provided some new concepts—resonance, entrainment, and pattern identification—to help you appreciate the subtle, yet powerful energies of sound.

With the recognition of the effect of the human soundscape comes a valuable side benefit: you will make better choices about the sounds that surround *all* your loved ones. This will be good for the entire family.

As discussed, canines are infinitely adaptable. This is what makes them our best friends. Although this resiliency bonds people and dogs, it can also be detrimental to animals' well-being. Dogs want so much to please us that they will suffer sensory insult way past the point we humans would. This may be one of the most important considerations we broach: to what degree do the increasing maladies and troubled behaviors of our dogs reflect our own difficulties? Our canines are adaptable; *we* are adamant about keeping up with the latest lifestyle changes and devices, lured by promises of more efficient lives. Most of us live with an unnatural amount of stress and keep adding more.

Through a Dog's Ear has been written with a very strong emphasis on the interconnection of the entire biosphere: people, animals, plants, and energy. It has long been known that resonance and entrainment, the processes where one vibration can alter another, have a powerful effect on humans. To clinically discover that our rhythms affect our dog pals is yet one more confirmation of the energetic linkage between all living things.

One could say that this book has also been a clandestine approach to educating people about the importance of healthy auditory function under the context of being a "dog book." The truth is that we can't deny our desire to bring peace and well-being into every household regardless of the portal through which we gratefully enter.

OLD FRIENDS

As we write these final pages, I recall my fascination with these furry creatures with cold noses when I was a tiny child. Can you remember the feeling of seeing your first dog? I remember thinking that not only had I found a perfect height-mate, but a living, breathing, smelly compatriot whom I could share my deepest secrets with and who wouldn't tell Mom (like my older sister would).

Now, fifty-plus years later, I sentimentally reflect on Davey Cocker, Noopie (couldn't quite say Snoopy), Obediah, and Lovely Rita. How well I got to know each of these beings—feeding, walking, and bathing them, picking up after them, teasing and berating them, playing with and loving them, and, for some, having the awesome responsibility and privilege of bringing them to the gate of passing Onwards.

I go for long stretches between dog pals. The heart stays tender for many years and I am not in a rush to replace the irreplaceable. —J. L.

As humans, we have such a tremendous responsibility for this world that we seemingly command. The broad implications of these dog studies are just another indicator of what the greatest sages have always taught: we are all connected.

As considerations of sustainability become ever more present, it is incumbent upon us to take the time to figure out what we do, how it affects everything around us, and what we will do to protect those that count on us.

Our animals have been longing to help us find the answers.

The Human-Animal Bond

Researching and coauthoring *Through a Dog's Ear* has been a true gift. I have learned so much about psychoacoustics and the benefit of a healthy sonic environment for my canine patients. The most exciting piece of this work, however, has been the realization that we now have a tool that can be used to help humans and animals heal together.

In this book, we have presented music applications that will enhance the well-being of both you and your animal companion. I also hope we have helped you understand the degree to which humans and animals are in this game of life together.

As a veterinarian, I have always understood the importance of animals in their guardians' lives. I have had clients whose only family was a dog or cat, and have witnessed the devastating grief over the loss of their sole companion. All of us who love animals know there is no such thing as *just* a dog, cat, or horse. I believe these four-legged spiritual beings are our teachers and our healers.

Research has shown that having an animal companion supports our physical and emotional health. One study revealed that patients diagnosed with heart disease were more likely to be alive one year later if they had a dog. (This was beyond any value from the increased exercise from walking the dogs.) This increased longevity was due to the healing power of the human-animal bond.[1] One of my dreams is to have a human *and* animal healing facility, because I believe that when more than one species heals together it creates a synergistic effect for each one.

Along these lines, I would like to end with the story of George and Gracie, one of my favorites. I love this story because it reflects the larger themes of the human-animal bond while also illustrating how music can help canines and their guardians get through difficult times.

Gracie is a beautiful akita with a huge heart. Her first year of life, however, was filled with abuse. She was rescued by a wonderful, caring family that has given her a fabulous home. Unfortunately, the previous abuse had taken its toll, and Gracie was left with fear aggression. Her family did everything they could from a conventional veterinary and behavioral perspective, but she still retained some aggressive tendencies. Because I had taken care of this family's other canine members for years, I asked if I could try energy therapy with Gracie. They were openminded (and openhearted) enough to try it. The energy sessions did wonders for Gracie—she acted like a puppy again.

Many months later, George (Gracie's guardian) underwent surgery, from which he suffered complications. Back home, he was in tremendous pain and was very ill. Gracie had never seen George behave like this, and the stress brought back her previous symptoms of fear aggression. George couldn't understand why Gracie didn't want to lie by his side, and he was crushed when she growled at him. To make matters worse, the post-surgical pain was preventing him from sleeping. Needless to say, it was a very stressful time for the two- and four-leggeds in the household.

Then a realization dawned on me. The calming music, created by Joshua and Lisa, that had been so helpful in my previous work with Gracie could now help *both* George and Gracie. His rest and healing would play a role in reducing her stress, and her return to a happy nature would help him on his road to recovery. How wonderful it was to have a tool that really supported the human-animal bond. To me, this was what the music study was really all about—animals and people healing together.

The most important piece of this story, however, is that the restoration of George and Gracie's relationship was essential for each of them to recover quickly. Gracie was on the verge of deteriorating to a very unhappy and unmanageable state of being, and George was doing poorly in a pain-altered world of frustration and sorrow.

George's wife, Tina, became the healing angel for them both. She didn't banish Gracie from the home—she understood exactly how important it was for George and Gracie to stay together. Her caring and calm nature kept it all from falling apart. Through intensive work by all involved, George and Gracie soon were helping each other heal. Gracie felt so much better seeing her guardian up and around, and George was buoyed by her constant companionship. The entire family got through this difficult time together. Whether it goes from person to animal, or animal to person, *nothing* heals like unconditional love.

—Dr. Susan Wagner
Columbus, Ohio
August 2007

About the Enclosed Starter CD

AS DISCUSSED THROUGHOUT the book, Joshua Leeds and Lisa Spector have created a series of clinically tested music CDs. These recordings are psychoacoustically designed to calm your canine *and* you—separately or together. There are two 20-minute tracks, each with a different function.

Track One contains four selections from the *Music to Calm Your Canine Companion* series, Vols. 1–2. These compositions reduce anxiety, and in many cases, relax dogs into sleep. The instrumentation is simple—solo piano. The individual pieces have been selected and/or rearranged to gradually reduce the heart rate. This is accomplished naturally by progressively slowing rhythms and simplifying auditory data. *Music to Calm Your Canine Companion* is recommended for when your dog is left alone or anxiety is anticipated—such as separation, thunderstorms, fireworks, or guests arriving. (*You* will also find it to be extremely relaxing. Just don't listen while operating heavy machinery.)

Track Two contains four selections from the *Music for the Canine Household* series. Given that dogs and people live together, there are times when you want your animal to relax without falling asleep yourself. This uplifting, psychoacoustically designed music can be played for the enjoyment and relaxation of people while simultaneously providing a positive sound environment for dogs. The clinically tested selections from *Music for the Canine Household* are a little more stimulating than the *Calm Your Canine* CD, with quicker tempos and more complex arrangements and orchestration.

RECOMMENDED USAGE

- Experiment: Given that people's response to music varies depending on time of day, how they feel physically and emotionally, and circadian rhythms, etc., we believe the same holds true with dogs. Therefore, we recommend experimenting with the two different tracks. See what happens. Track One is designed to sooth; Track Two is designed to be uplifting.
- Volume: Keep pleasant and gentle.
- Dosage: Given that this music is a natural remedy, you do not have to be concerned with dosage and frequency. Concern for harm is unnecessary as long as no one eats the CD.
- More detailed instructions for the use of *Through a Dog's Ear* CDs can be found in chapters 9 and 10.

COMPOSITIONS

- Track One—*Music to Calm Your Canine Companion* (23 minutes)

    Instrumentation: Piano

    Prelude in C Major / Bach

    Foreign Lands / Schumann

    Vocalise / Rachmaninoff

    Reverie / Debussy

- Track Two—*Music for the Canine Household* (18 minutes)

    Instrumentation: Oboe, cello, piano

    Serenade / Schubert

    Intermezzo in A / Brahms

    Cello Sonata in D / Mendelssohn

    Prelude in D / Bach

The Apollo Chamber Ensemble

Piano: Lisa Spector

Oboe: Barbara Midney

Cello: Sarah Fiene (Schubert), Tanya Tomkins (Mendelssohn)

Producer: Joshua Leeds

For more information about the *Through a Dog's Ear* music series and additional music recommendations, visit ThroughADogsEar.com.

BioAcoustic Research and Development (BARD)

BIOACOUSTICS, SIMPLY PUT, is the study of the sounds that animals make—how they produce it and how they use it to communicate. A broader definition includes the exploration of the effect of the human soundscape upon animals.

BioAcoustic Research & Development is a unique partnership of musician Lisa Spector and sound researcher Joshua Leeds. With Lisa's deep knowledge of the Western classical repertoire and her lifetime love affair with dogs, she is the inspiration for BARD. Joshua Leeds has an interest in all things sonic and vibrating.

BARD is research-centric and practical in application. Its mission is to provide audio programs specifically for the health, well-being, and longevity of our beloved animal friends.

Resources

BEHAVIOR

American College of Veterinary Behaviorists (ACVB)
www.dacvb.org
These are veterinarians who have a special interest in behavior problems or who are board-certified in animal behavior.

American Veterinary Society of Animal Behavior (AVSAB)
www.avsabonline.org
This organization and site offers the excellent document, "How to Choose a Trainer."

The Animal Behavior Society (ABS)

Indiana University

2611 East 10th Street

Bloomington, IN 47408-2603

812-856-5541

www.animalbehavior.org

The ABS promotes the study of animal behavior, with members that study this discipline from all over the world.

www.animalbehavior.net

800-372-3706

You can also ask a veterinary behavior technician questions by calling their toll-free line.

www.CertifiedAnimalBehaviorist.com

This website will help you find an Animal Behavior Society certified behaviorist near you. These are professionals with advanced training in behavior, and can work with you and your veterinarian.

Indoor Cat Initiative

http://vet.osu.edu/indoorcat

This website gives helpful tips on feline wellness.

*150 Activites for Bored Dogs: Surefire Ways to Keep Your Dog
Active and Happy*
Sue Owens Wright
Avon, MA: Adam's Media, 2007
*We recommend this book because it is filled with positive activities for
your canine companion.*

VETERINARY INTEGRATIVE MEDICINE

The Academy of Veterinary Homeopathy (AVH)
PO Box 9280
Wilmington, DE 19809
866-652-1590
www.theavh.org
*Learn more about veterinary homeopathy and find a professional
near you.*

American Holistic Veterinary Medical Association
Dr. Carvel G. Tiekert, Executive Director
2218 Old Emmorton Road
Bel Air, MD 21015
410-569-0795
www.ahvma.org
*You can learn about complementary and alternative veterinary care,
and find a holistic veterinarian near you.*

American Veterinary Chiropractic Association (AVCA)

442154 East 140 Road

Bluejacket, OK 74333

918-784-2231

www.animalchiropractic.org

Learn about veterinary chiropractic and find a certified doctor near you.

Healing Touch for Animals™

Komitor Healing Method, Inc. (HTA/KHM)

PO Box 63217

Highlands Ranch, CO 80163-2177

866-470-6572

www.healingtouchforanimals.com

HTA/KHM are energy techniques that promote healing and energy balance. The founder, Carol Komitor, combined her expertise in human energy healing with her knowledge as a veterinary technician to develop this modality.

International Association of Animal Massage and Bodywork (IAAMB)

Marcia Meeker, Coordinator

3347 McGregor Lane

Toledo, OH 43623

800-903-9350

www.iaamb.org

Learn about animal massage and bodywork and find a professional near you.

International Veterinary Acupuncture Society (IVAS)

PO Box 271395

Ft. Collins, CO 80527-1395

970-266-0666

www.ivas.org

IVAS is an organization dedicated to promoting excellence in veterinary acupuncture. This website will help you find a veterinary acupuncturist near you.

Reconnective Healing™

PO Box 3600

Hollywood, CA 90078-3600

888-374-2732

www.TheReconnection.com

Investigated in scientific laboratories, Reconnective Healing is a modality that connects the animal or person to a universal healing frequency.

The Veterinary Botanical Medicine Association (VBMA)

Jasmine C. Lyon, Executive Director

1785 Poplar Drive

Kennesaw, GA 30144

office@vbma.org

www.vbma.org

Learn about herbal medicine for animals and find a professional near you.

INTEGRATIVE MEDICINE (FOR PEOPLE)

Benson-Henry Institute for Mind Body Medicine
824 Boylston Street
Chestnut Hill, MA 02467
617-732-9130
www.mbmi.org
The Benson-Henry Institute is doing cutting edge research in the area of mind-body medicine.

Consortium of Academic Health Centers for Integrative Medicine
(CAHCIM)
D513 Mayo, Mail Code 505
420 Delaware Street SE
Minneapolis, MN 55455
612-624-9166
www.imconsortium.org
This group of academic institutions is transforming healthcare through research, education, and clinical programs in integrative medicine.

National Center for Complementary and Alternative Medicine
(NCCAM)
9000 Rockville Pike
Bethesda, MA 20892
http://nccam.nih.gov
NCCAM is a part of the National Institutes of Health, and offers an informative newsletter in the area of complementary and alternative medicine and research.

Andrew Weil, MD

www.drweil.com, www.healthyaging.com

Dr. Weil is a leading pioneer in integrative medicine.

Your-Center

www.your-center.com

This website contains excellent information on integrative medicine.

ANIMAL ADVOCACY ORGANIZATIONS

American Humane Association

63 Inverness Drive East

Englewood, CO 80112

303-792-9900

www.americanhumane.org

American Society for the Prevention of Cruelty to

Animals (ASPCA)

424 E. 92nd Street

New York, NY 10128-6804

212-876-7700

www.aspca.org

The Animal Health Foundation
5576 Corporate Avenue
Cypress, CA 90630
www.animalhealthfoundation.net

The Association of Veterinarians for Animal Rights (AVAR)
PO Box 208
Davis, CA 95617-0208
530-759.8106
www.avar.org
*This association of veterinarians works toward the acquisition of rights
for all non-human animals by educating the public and the veterinary
profession about a variety of issues concerning non-human animal use.
The AVAR actively seeks reformation of the way society treats all non-
humans and an increase in environmental awareness, as well.*

Deaf Dog Education Action Fund
PO Box 2840
Oneco, FL 34264-2840
www.deafdogs.org

Humane Society of the United States
2100 L Street NW
Washington, DC 20037
202-452-1100
www.hsus.org

The National Resource Center on the Link Between Violence to
People and Animals
American Humane Association
800-227-4645 x461
www.americanhumane.org

ANIMAL-ASSISTED THERAPY AND ANIMAL-ASSISTED ACTIVITIES

www.animaltherapy.net
*This website offers distance learning in animal-assisted therapy
and activities.*

Delta Society
875 124th Avenue NE, #101
Bellevue, WA 98005
425-679-5500
www.DeltaSociety.org
*The Delta Society is a leading organization in establishing standards
for animal-assisted therapy.*

The Good Dog Foundation
607 Sixth Street
Brooklyn, NY 11215
888-859-9992
www.thegooddogfoundation.org
This organization is dedicated to all aspects of animal-assisted therapy, from training and certification to visitation and support.

Green Chimneys
400 Doansburg Road, Box 719
Brewster, NY 10509
845-279-2995
www.greenchimneys.org
Green Chimneys is a worldwide leader in the area of animal-assisted therapy for children with emotional, behavioral, or learning challenges.

Guide Dogs for the Blind
350 Los Ranchitos Road
San Rafael, CA 94903
415-499-4000
www.guidedogs.com
It was through a loving Guide Dog puppy-in-training that Through a Dog's Ear *was conceptualized.*

Therapet

www.therapet.com

Therapet offers animal-assisted therapy and Healing Through Touch for rehabilitation patients.

4-H PetPALS

The Ohio State University Extension, 4-H Development

www.4hpetpals.osu.edu

This organization combines children, animals, and the elderly in a healing partnership.

PSYCHOACOUSTICS, HEARING, AND NOISE POLLUTION

House Ear Institute

2100 W. 3rd Street

Los Angeles, CA 90057

213-483-4431

www.hei.org

A non-profit organization dedicated to advancing hearing science through research and education to improve quality of life.

Noise Pollution Clearinghouse

PO Box 1137

Montpelier VT 05601-1137

888-200-8332

www.nonoise.org

The mission of the Noise Pollution Clearinghouse is to create more civil cities and more natural rural and wilderness areas by reducing noise pollution at the source.

ThePowerOfSound.com, Sound-Remedies.com

Websites of Joshua Leeds with information about the effect of music and sound on the human nervous system.

World Forum for Acoustic Ecology (US Chapter)

www.acousticecology.org/asae

The American Society for Acoustic Ecology (ASAE) is dedicated to exploring the role of sound in natural habitats and human societies, and promoting public dialogue concerning the identification, preservation, and restoration of natural and cultural sound environments.

FRIENDS OF *THROUGH A DOG'S EAR*

Ace Dog Sports

Sandy Rogers, Director

San Francisco and Pacifica, CA

www.acedogsports.com

Teaches people how to handle their dogs for a variety of goals, specializing in relationship building, bonding, balancing, and agility training.

Camp Unleashed
Annie Brody, Director
PO Box 410
West Stockbridge, MA 01266
518-781-0446
www.campunleashed.com
Camp Unleashed is a retreat in the countryside dedicated to honoring and respecting the spirit of dogs in the community of like-minded souls, both human and canine.

Lisa Spector's Music School
80-Q N. Cabrillo Hwy., #228
Half Moon Bay, CA 94019
650-726-5119
www.LisaSpector.com
The mission of Lisa Spector's Music School is to educate with joy and encouragement, to create a nurturing environment for musical expression, and to promote music awareness in the community.

Pet Pause
Sue Raimond, Director
PO Box 1242
Pine Valley, CA 91962
800-971-1044
www.petpause2000.com
Sue Raimond is an extraordinary pioneer of harp enrichment/therapy for wild and domesticated animals.

Notes

INTRODUCTION: A NEW SOUND AWARENESS

1. Barbara Sherman Simpson. "Approaches to Canine Behavior Management in Canine Behavior Problems: A Four Step Approach." Advanstar Communications Inc., 2007: 6–8.
2. Newsbriefs. *Veterinary Forum* 24, no. 5 (May 2007): 14.
3. Angus Phillips, "A Love Story; Our Bond with Dogs," *National Geographic,* January 2002, 22.
4. *Webster's Third New International Dictionary* (Springfield, MA: Merriam-Webster, Inc., 1993), 1832.
5. For people, the ability to *listen actively* facilitates the loop of language, education, communication, and social interaction. There is no aspect of normal living—home, family, or employment—that is not dependent on these skills.
6. Resonance, entrainment, and pattern identification form the foundation upon which most sound therapies are built. Advanced approximation of these principles include binaural

beat frequencies, filtration/gating, and harmonic re-tunings. For further information, visit the website of Joshua Leeds: www.ThePowerOfSound.com.

7. The Acoustical Society of America, http://asa.aip.org/ani_bioac/index.html.

8. *Webster's Third New International Dictionary,* 218.

9. D. L. Wells, L. Graham, and P. G. Hepper, "The Influence of Auditory Stimulation on the Behaviour of Dogs Housed in a Rescue Shelter," *Animal Welfare* 11 (2002): 385–393.

10. The first four albums recorded by Lisa Spector and Joshua Leeds were released in 2006. Entitled *Calm* and *Uplifting,* they are a part of the Essential Sound Series. Detailed information can be found at www.EssentialSoundSeries.com.

CHAPTER 1: PETEY, SHUT UP!

1. "Lover, Come Back to Me" was written by Oscar Hammerstein II and Sigmund Romburg in 1928.

2. Deaf Dog Education Action Fund, PO Box 2840, Oneco, FL 34264-2840, www.deafdogs.org.

3. Malcolm R. Gamble, "Sound and Its Significance for Laboratory Animals," *Biological Review* 57 (1982): 395–421.

4. Dr. Alfred Tomatis was born in France and lived from 1920–2001.

5. Susan L. Stapes, "Human Response to Environmental Noise," *American Psychologist* 51, no. 2 (1996): 143–150.

6. Rick Weiss, "Noise Pollution Takes Toll on Health and Happiness: Everyday Noise Can Overstimulate the Body's Stress Response," *Washington Post,* June 5, 2007.

7. Karen E. Lange, "The Human-Dog Connection," *National Geographic,* January 2002, 4.

8. The Monks of New Skete, *How to be Your Dog's Best Friend* (New York: Little, Brown & Company, 2002), 153–154.

CHAPTER 2:
THE EFFECT OF SOUND ON INHABITANTS OF YOUR HOME

1. The stapedius and tensor tympani muscles, located in the middle ear, are actually so small that they are not included in most textbook drawings of the ear.

2. Temple Grandin, *Animals in Translation: Using the Mysteries of Autism to Decode Animal Behavior* (New York: Scribner, 2005), 49.

3. Robert Kubey and Mihaly Csikszentmihalyi, "Television Addiction is No Mere Metaphor," *Scientific American,* February 2002, 76–80.

CHAPTER 3: ADAPTABLE DOGS

1. Malcolm Gamble, "Sound and Its Significance for Laboratory Animals," 395–421.

2. Herbert Benson, Benson-Henry Institute for Mind Body Medicine, 824 Boylston Street, Chestnut Hill, MA 02467, www.mbmi.org.

CHAPTER 4: OWNERSHIP OR PARTNERSHIP?

1. Rupert Sheldrake, *Dogs That Know When Their Owners Are Coming Home* (New York: Three Rivers Press, 1999), 16.
2. *Webster's Third New International Dictionary,* 1171.

CHAPTER 5: THOROUGHLY MODERN DOGS

1. Sound is the primary focus in *Through a Dog's Ear.* However, in assessing your dog's sensory quotient, other sensory stimulants should be taken into account as well.
2. According to the National Institute on Deafness and Other Communication Disorders, 85 dB (for a period of eight hours) is the level at which hearing damage begins. No more than fifteen minutes of unprotected exposure is recommended for sounds between 90–100 dB. Regular exposure to sound over 100 dB for more than one minute risks permanent hearing loss. The threshold of physical sensation begins around 120 dB. The threshold of pain begins around 125 dB. Further information can be found online at www.nidcd.nih.gov/health/.
3. National Institute on Deafness and Other Communication Disorders, http://www.nidcd.nih.gov/health/education/teachers/common_sounds.asp.
4. The Monks of New Skete, *How to Be Your Dog's Best Friend,* 158.

CHAPTER 6:
WHY MUSIC AFFECTS YOU AND YOUR CANINE COMPANION

1. Wells, Graham, and Hepper, "The Influence of Auditory Stimulation on the Behaviour of Dogs Housed in a Rescue Shelter," 385–393.

2. *Through a Dog's Ear: Music to Calm Your Canine Companion* is the first in a series of recordings published by Sounds True. Clinically demonstrated in tests with over 150 dogs in shelters, service dog organizations, clinics, groomers, and homes, the music on these recordings has been shown to deeply calm and reduce anxiety in dogs. Test results can be found at www.ThroughADogsEar.com.

CHAPTER 7: BREAKTHROUGH RESEARCH

1. Alfred Tomatis, *The Conscious Ear* (New York: Station Hill Press, 1991), 186.

2. Wells, Graham, and Hepper, "The Influence of Auditory Stimulation on the Behaviour of Dogs Housed in a Rescue Shelter," 385–393.

3. *Webster's Third New International Dictionary,* 2244.

4. Pierre Sollier, *Listening for Wellness* (Walnut Creek, CA: The Mozart Center Press, 2005), 63–66.

CHAPTER 8: ABOUT YOUR DOG'S BEHAVIOR

1. A. Kaffman and M. J. Meaney, "Neurodevelopmental Sequelae of Postnatal Maternal Care in Rodents: Clinical and Research Implication of Molecular Insights," *Journal of Child Psychology and Psychiatry* 48, no. 3–4 (2007): 224–244.

2. Zhang, et al., "Maternal Programming of Defensive Responses Through Sustained Effects on Gene Expression," *Biological Psychology* 73 (2006): 72–89.

3. Between 4,000–6,000 animal shelters exist in the United States with 6–8 million cats and dogs entering shelters each year. (Human Society of the U.S., October, 2006).

4. Lilly Behavior Symposium, 2.

5. Deborah Wells, "Aromatherapy for Travel-induced Excitement in Dogs," *Journal of the American Veterinary Medical Association* 229, no. 6 (September 15, 2006): 964–967.

6. The extraordinary work of Don Carlson and his Sonic Bloom research and practices are well described in the following article: Michael Spillane, "Brave New Waves," *Tender Loving Care for Plants,* Spring 1991.

CHAPTER 9:
USING MUSIC AND SOUND FOR BEHAVIORAL ISSUES

1. Gary Landsberg, Wayne H. Whithausen, and Lowell Ackerman, *Handbook of Behavior Problems of the Dog and Cat* (London: Elgerier, 2003), 385–426.

2. *Music for Driving* is part of the *Music for the Canine Household* series. Further information and online sales are available at ThroughADogsEar.com.

CHAPTER 10: LIVING A BETTER LIFE TOGETHER

1. MayoClinic.com, November 9, 2005.
2. J.L. Westropp and C. A. Buffington, "Feline Idiopathic Cystitis: Current Understanding of Pathophysiology and Management," *Veterinary Clinics of North America—Small Animal Practice* 34 (2004): 1043–1055.

EPILOGUE

1. E. Friedmann and S.A. Thomas, "Pet Ownership, Social Support, and One Year Survival After Acute Myocardial Infarction in the Cardiac Arrhythmia Suppression Trial," *American Journal of Cardiology* 76 (1995): 1213–1217.

References

Andrews, T. *Animal-Wise: The Spirit Language and Signs of Nature.* Jackson, TN: Dragonhawk Publishing, 1999.

_____. *Animal Speak: The Spiritual & Magical Powers of Creatures Great & Small.* Woodbury, MN: Llewellyn Publications, 1993.

Beerda, et al. "Chronic Stress in Dogs Subjected to Social and Spatial Restriction." *Physiology & Behavior.* 66, no.2 (April 1999): 243–254.

Bell, K. L. *Holistic Aromatherapy for Animals.* Scotland: Findhorn Press, 2002.

Buckley, J. P. "Physiological effects of environmental stimuli." *Journal of Pharmaceutical Sciences.* 61, no.8 (August 1972).

Covell, V. *Spirit Animals.* Nevada City, CA: Dawn Publications, 2000.

Crawford, J. and K. Pomerinke. *Therapy Pets: The Animal-Human Healing Partnership.* Amherst, NY: Prometheus Books, 2003.

Draper, T. W. "Canine Analogs of Human Personality Factors." *Journal of General Psychology.* 122, no. 3 (July 1995): 241–252.

Espe, M. *Whispers of Heaven: Excerpts from the Animals' Voice.* Collierville, TN: InstantPublishers.com, 2004.

Fuller, J. L., et al., "Genotype and Behavioral Vulnerability to Isolation in Dogs." *Journal of Comparative and Physiological Psychology.* 66, no. 1 (1968): 151–156.

Gamble, M. R. "Sound and Its Significance for Laboratory Animals." *Biological Review 57.* (1982): 395–421.

Gerber, R. *A Practical Guide to Vibrational Medicine: Energy Healing and Spiritual Transformation.* New York: Quill, 2001.

Goldstein, M. *The Nature of Animal Healing: The Definitive Holistic Medicine Guide to Caring for Your Dog and Cat.* New York: Ballantine Books, 1999.

Grandin, T. *Animals in Translation: Using the Mysteries of Autism to Decode Animal Behavior.* New York: Scribner, 2005.

Gray, P. M., et al. "Enhanced: The Music of Nature and the Nature of Music." *Science Online.* 291, no. 5501. (January 5, 2001): 52–54.

Grogan, John. *Marley & Me.* New York: HarperCollins, 2005.

Gue, M. "Stress-induced Changes in Gastric Emptying, Postprandial Motility, and Plasma Gut Hormone Levels in Dogs." *Gastroenterology.* 97, no. 5 (November 1997): 1101–1107.

Hessler-Key, M. *What Animals Teach Us: Love, Loyalty, Heroism, and Other life Lessons from Our Pets.* New York: Prima Publishing, 2001.

Houpt, K. et al., A Preliminary Study of the Effect of Music on Equine Behavior. *Journal of Equine Veterinary Science* 20, no. 11 (2000).

Houston, J. *Mystical Dogs*. Maui, HI: Inner Ocean Publishing, 2002.

Izumi, A. "Japanese Monkeys Perceive Sensory Consonance of Chords." *Journal of Acoustical Society America 108*, no. 6 (December 2000): 3073–3078.

Carlson, S. et al. "Effects of Music and Noise on Working Memory Performance in Monkeys." *Neuroreport* 8, no. 13 (September 8, 1997): 2853–2856.

Kaffman, A., and M. J. Meaney. "Neurodevelopmental Sequelae of Postnatal Maternal Care in Rodents: Clinical and Research Implication of Molecular Insights." *Journal of Child Psychology and Psychiatry* 48, no. 3-4 (2007): 224–244.

Kempf, et al., "The Effects of Aircraft Noise on Wildlife." *Journal Fuer Ornithologie* 137, no. 1 (1996): 101–113.

Kubey, R., and M. Csikszentmihalyi. "Television Addicition Is No Mere Metaphor." *Scientific American,* February 2002, 76–80.

Ladd, J. K., et al. "Behavioral and Physiological Studies on the Effect of Music on Animals." *Journal of Animal Science* 70, no. 1 (1992).

Landsberg, G. *"Diagnosing and Treating Separation Anxiety."* Lilly Behavior Symposium, Advanstar Communications, Inc., 2007, p. 2.

Lange, K. "The Human-Dog Connection." *National Geographic,* January 2002, p. 4.

Leeds, J. *Sonic Alchemy: Conversations with Leading Sound Practitioners*. San Rafael, CA: InnerSong Press, 1997.

_____. *The Power of Sound: How to Manage Your Personal Soundscape for a Vital, Productive, and Healthy Life.* Rochester, VT: Healing Arts Press, 2001.

Lozanov, G. *Suggestology and Outlines of Suggestopedy.* New York: Gordon and Breach Science Publishers, 1978.

Margoliash, D. *"The Song Does Not Remain the Same."* Science 291, no. 5513 (2001): 2559–2561.

Masson, J. M. *Dogs Never Lie About Love.* New York: Three Rivers Press, 1998.

_____. *When Elephants Weep.* New York: Dell Publishing, 1995.

McCarthy, D. O., et al. "The Effects of Noise Stress on Leukocyte in Rats." *Research in Nursing Health* 15, no. 2 (April 1992): 131–137.

McConnell, P. B. *For the Love of a Dog.* New York: Ballantine Books, 2005.

McCormick, A., and M. McCormick. *Horse Sense and the Human Heart: What Horses Teach Us About Trust, Bonding, Creativity and Spirituality.* Deerfield Beach, FL: HealthCommunications Inc., 1997.

Milligan, S. R., et al. "Sound Levels in Rooms Housing Laboratory Animals: An Uncontrolled Daily Variable." *Physiology & Behavior* 53, no. 6 (1993): 1067–1076.

The Monks of New Skete. *How to Be Your Dog's Best Friend.* New York: Little, Brown & Company, 2002.

Moore, D. "Postnatal Development of Mammalian Central Auditory System and the Neural Consequences of Auditory Deprivation." *Acta Otolaryngology Supplement* 421 (1985): 19–30.

Neilson, J. "How I Treat Food-Related Aggression in Dogs." *Veterinary Medicine* 102, no. 4 (April 2007): 247–252.

Newberry, R. C. "Environmental Enrichment: Increasing the Biological Relevance of Captive Environments." *Applied Animal Behavior Science* 44 (1995): 229–243.

Nunez, M. J., et al. "Music, Immunity and Cancer." *Life Sciences* 71, no. 9 (July 19, 2002): 1047–1057.

Oschman, J. *Energy Medicine: The Scientific Basis.* London: Churchill Livingstone, 2000.

Oliver, P. "Sonic Bloom: Music to Plantís Stomata?" *Countryside & Small Stock Journal* 86 (July/August 2002), 74.

Owens, P., with N. Eckroate. *The Dog Whisperer: A Compassionate, Nonviolent Approach to Dog Training,* 2nd. Avons, MA: Adams Media, 2007, 2–5.

Page, J. *Dogs: A Natural History.* New York: Smithsonian Books, 2007.

Panksepp, J., et al. "Emotional Sounds and the Brain: The Neuro-Affective Foundations of Musical Appreciation." *Behavioral Processes* 60: 133–155.

Rajan, R. "Unilateral Hearing Losses Alter Loud Sound-Induced Temporary Threshold Shifts and Efferent Effects in the Normal-Hearing Ear." *Journal of Neurophysiology* 85, no. 3 (March 2001): 1257–1269.

Reisner, I. R. "Assessment, Management, and Prognosis of Canine Dominance-Related Aggression." *Veterinary Clinics of North America—Small Animal Practice* 27, no. 3 (May 1997): 479–495.

Schapiro, H., et al. "Sensory Deprivation on Visceral Activity: The Effect of Auditory and Vestibular Deprivation on Canine Gastric Secretion." *Psychosomatic Medicine* 32, no. 5 (September 1970): 515–521.

Schieber, B. *Nose to Nose: A Memoir of Healing.* Seeley Lake, MT: Silent Moon Books, 2002.

Schoen, A., and S. Wynn. *Complementary and Alternative Veterinary Medicine: Principles and Practice.* St. Louis, MO: Mosby, 1998.

Schoen, A. *Kindred Spirits: How the Remarkable Bond Between Human & Animals Can Change The Way We Live.* New York: Broadway Books, 2001.

Schwartz, C. *Four Paws Five Directions: A Guide to Chinese Medicine for Cats and Dogs.* Berkeley, CA: Celestial Arts, 1996.

Schwartz, G., and L. Schwartz. *The Living Energy Universe: A Fundamental Discovery That Transforms Science & Medicine.* Charlottesville, VA: Hampton Roads Publishing Company Inc., 1999.

Simpson, B. S. "Canine Communication." *Veterinary Clinics of North America—Small Animal Practice* 27, no. 3 (May 1997): 445–464.

Sheldrake, R. *Dogs That Know When Their Owners Are Coming Home.* New York: Three Rivers Press, 1999.

Smith, J. *Animal Communication: Our Sacred Connection.* Lakeville, MN: Galde Press Inc., 2005.

Staccia, C. *Diabetes Living: The Will to Be Well.* Ashland, OH: Atlas Books, 2007.

Stapes, S. L. "Human Response to Environmental Noise." *American Psychologist* 51, no. 2 (Febuary 1996): 143–50.

Tomatis, A. *The Conscious Ear. New York:* Station Hill Press, 1991.

Weiss, R. "Noise Pollution Takes Toll on Health and Happiness: Everyday Noise Can Overstimulate the Bodyís Stress Response." *Washington Post,* June 5, 2007.

Wells, D. L., et al. "The Influence of Environmental Change on the Behavior of Sheltered Dogs." *Applied Animal Behaviour Science* 68 (2000): 151–162.

_____. "A Note on the Influence of Visual Conspecific Contact on the Behaviour of Sheltered Dogs." *Applied Animal Behaviour* 60, no.1 (October 1998): 83–88.

_____. "Aromatherapy as Enrichment for Kenneled Dogs." Canine Behavior Centre, School of Psychology, Queen's University Belfast, BT7 1NN United Kingdom.

Wells, D. L., L. Graham, and P. G. Hepper. "The Influence of Auditory Stimulation on the Behaviour of Dogs Housed in a Rescue Shelter." *Animal Welfare* 11 (2002): 385–393.

_____. "Aromatherapy for Travel-Induced Excitement in Dogs." *Journal of the American Veterinary Medical Association* 229, no. 6 (September 15, 2006): 964–967.

Westropp, J. L., and C. A. Buffington. Feline Idiopathic Cystitis: Current Understanding of Pathophysiology and Management. *Veterinary Clinics of North America—Small Animal Practice* 34 (2004): 1043–1055.

Wynn, S. *Manual of Natural Veterinary Medicine: Science and Tradition.* St. Louis, MO: Mosby, 2003.

Zhang et al. "Maternal Programming of Defensive Responses Through Sustained Effects on Gene Expression." *Biological Psychology* 73 (2006): 72–89.

ThroughADogsEar.com

WE HOPE THAT by reading this book you are now more aware of the effect of our human sounds on the well-being of the dogs who live with us. This is only the beginning of our conversation. Please join us online to stay abreast of new research, new products, and ways to connect to other conscious canine guardians.

At ThroughADogsEar.com you will find:

- Latest dog/music research
- Music recommendations for the entire canine household
- Tips on the use of music for calming canine behavioral issues
- Free music downloads
- Music samples, including:
  Music to Calm Your Canine Companion
  Music for the Canine Household
  Music for Driving with Your Dog

- Sound suggestions from Dr. Susan Wagner and other animal professionals
- More about the evolving fields of psychoacoustics and bioacoustics
- Additional unpublished material from *Through a Dog's Ear*
- Your stories of dogs and music
- Online purchase of music and books
- Special offers

About the
Authors

Joshua Leeds is a sound researcher, music producer, and educator. He is one of few published authorities in the field of *psychoacoustics*—the study of the effects of music and sound on the human

Dominic with Joshua Leeds

nervous system. Prior publications include *The Power of Sound* (Healing Arts Press, 2001) and *Sonic Alchemy* (InnerSong Press, 1997). Collaborating with leaders in health, psychology, and neurodevelopment, Joshua's application-specific soundtracks are used around the world.

Residing in the San Francisco Bay area, Joshua presents seminars internationally to music, healthcare, and education professionals. Further information can be found online at ThePowerOfSound.com.

Susan Wagner, DVM, MS, of Columbus, Ohio, is a respected veterinary neurologist whose current work emphasizes the importance

Susan Wagner with Kinsey and Oz

of the human-animal bond. Dr. Wagner practices and teaches veterinary integrative medicine and is adjunct faculty at The Ohio State University Veterinary College. For further information visit www.HumanAndAnimalHealing.com.

About
Sounds True

SOUNDS TRUE WAS founded in 1985 with a clear vision: to disseminate spiritual wisdom. Located in Boulder, Colorado, Sounds True publishes teaching programs that are designed to educate, uplift, and inspire. We work with many of the leading spiritual teachers, thinkers, healers, and visionary artists of our time.

To receive a free catalog of tools and teachings for personal and spiritual transformation, please visit www.soundstrue.com, call toll-free 800-333-9185, or write to us at the address below.

The Sounds True Catalog
PO Box 8010
Boulder, CO 80306

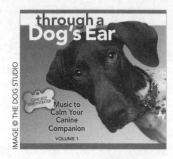

Music to Calm Your Canine Companion, Vol.1

AVAILABLE FROM SOUNDS TRUE

A 60-minute CD of classical music specifically arranged for the canine nervous system. Clinically demonstrated in homes and shelters to help relax dogs, reduce stress, and decrease separation and other anxiety disorders.

Music for the Canine Household, Vol. 1

AVAILABLE FROM BIOACOUSTIC RESEARCH & DEVELOPMENT

A selection of psychoacoustically designed classics engaging for human enjoyment, yet soothing enough to keep your dog relaxed and serene.

Music for Driving with Your Dog

AVAILABLE FROM BIOACOUSTIC RESEARCH & DEVELOPMENT

For dogs who become nervous or over-stimulated in the car, this CD features a balanced selection of classic compositions to help the driver stay alert while the canine passenger enjoys a tranquil ride.

Further information and online sales: **ThroughADogsEar.com**